Praise from Readers of *Millionaire by halftime*

"Millionaire by halftime is a refreshing playbook for building a successful network marketing business. As a former swimming coach, I love the analogies Presley uses between the discipline and dedication in sports and our profession. This book is packed with practical advice and exercises, and I'm going to use it with my team. I highly recommend this book!"

—Donna Johnson, Cave Creek, AZ

"Millionaire by halftime gives the essential fundamentals needed to achieve the life you've always wanted. Master these basics, and you will be the master of your future!"

—Diana Hightower, Garland, TX

"Presley's Millionaire by halftime is loaded with wisdom, common sense, and everyday practicality. It's a road map for success!"

—Noreen Savage, Doylestown, PA

"Millionaire by halftime is a must-read book for success seekers. Do you want to know what to do? Do you want to know what it takes? It's all here!"

—Michael Prettyman, Columbia, MD

"Presley Swagerty is a self-made success story. I discovered his walk is really no different than mine, and I would be foolish not to take advantage of the tips for success shared throughout this MUST-READ book."

—Kenny Kramer, Mechanicsburg, PA

"It's not often that reading material comes along that is so succinct in helping you understand what success truly is, but Millionaire by halftime was the perfect blueprint for my life."

—Bryan Childers, Dublin, GA

"Millionaire by halftime is an absolute game-changer!"

"If you want a roadmap for success, read this

—H(

D1306379

MILLIONAIRE

by

halftime

MILLIONAIRE
by
halftime

How to Win with Network Marketing

Presley Swagerty

NETWORKING Times
MOVING THE HEART OF BUSINESS PRESS

Published by Networking Times Press.

Distributed by Networking Times.

For ordering information or special discounts for bulk purchases, please contact:

Networking Times
11418 Kokopeli Place
Chatsworth, CA 91311
818-727-2000
www.networkingtimes.com.

Composition by Accelerate Media Partners LLC, Asheville, NC.

Cover design by Accelerate Media Partners LLC, Asheville, NC.

ISBN 13: 978-1-934550-04-5

Printed in the United States of America.

To my late mother, Lois Swagerty—you were the most Godly, loving woman I have ever known, and I am the man I am because of you. I miss you.

Contents

Foreword 1

Introduction. 3

Chapter 1 – Your Life Is the Big Leagues 7

Chapter 2 – The Network Marketing Profession 13

Chapter 3 – If You Want More, You Must Become More. 21

Chapter 4 – Get Out of Your Comfort Zone 31

Chapter 5 – Dream Big. No, Bigger!. 39

Chapter 6 – Stepping Stones to Your Dreams 45

Chapter 7 – Hard Work and Perseverance Pay Off 57

Chapter 8 – Start Now! 69

Chapter 9 – Finding the Right People. 75

Chapter 10 – Seven Uses of Social Media 87

Chapter 11 – Four Steps to Setting Appointments 97

Chapter 12 – Have Fun with 1-on-1s and 2-on-1s. 105

Chapter 13 – Awesome Home and Hotel Events 111

Chapter 14 – Websites and Webinars 121

Chapter 15 – The Fortune Is in the Follow Up. 127

Chapter 16 – How to Overcome Rejection 133

Chapter 17 – Obtain Huge Results Quickly 143

Chapter 18 – Team Building 101 151

Chapter 19 – Every Team Needs a Captain. 173

Epilogue 183

Coach's Q & A 187

Your Game Plan Reading List. 191

Acknowledgments 193

About the Author 195

Foreword

I'm proud to call Presley Swagerty my best friend. I feel blessed to say he is truly my brother in every way . . . we just had different mothers. Presley has been there for me in good times and bad times. He has mentored me and empowered me more than he will ever realize. I am proud that the Coach is my brother in Christ. He is a strong, dedicated Christian man. We have both stumbled and failed more than we would like to admit, but Presley was a faithful, exemplary son, a phenomenal father, and a committed, giving husband. I admire Jeanie for her unwavering dedication and support as a partner and spouse. I am honored to have the Swagertys as friends!

However, I had real trouble with Presley's request: "Bubba, I quote you in the book, so just give me a paragraph or two . . . I can't do the book without something from you." My apprehension was not my lack of something to share; those who know me can attest to the fact that I always have something to say. I read the draft of this powerful, insightful, and life-changing book and wondered what I could add of value. Jeanie and Presley have supported me and believed in me, even when I didn't believe in myself. I owe them so much. I wanted to contribute and was truly honored that I was asked, but what could I offer?

Then it hit me. What is the one question I am asked the most about the Coach, Presley Swagerty? I have been asked hundreds, if not thousands, of times what his secret is or for the answer to how he has accomplished so much. "What is the ONE thing that has made Presley so successful?"

Presley certainly has the dedication, perseverance, commitment, and vision this book teaches and promotes. We have all watched his personal growth and development explode. While his leadership skills have always been present, he has experienced an amazing expansion and maturity in his leadership that few accomplish. The Coach has never been afraid of hard work; he works harder than most folks I know. Presley has never forgotten his beliefs and core values. He is fair, honest, kind, and very patient. He has the gifts of diplomacy and compassion. Presley always strives to be a helper, supporter, and encourager to those around him. He is a giver of himself and whatever God has blessed him with.

However, if I could pick only one thing that has made Presley Swagerty successful, it would have to be his attitude. Your attitude is yours. You constantly choose whether you are going to control your thoughts and your attitude, or whether you will allow circumstances or someone else to control it. The great thing is that you get to decide. The Coach has control and mastery of his attitude.

He always sees the glass as half full. We are all given the same glass, and we all have the same amount in our glass, but we get to choose whether we see the glass as half full or half empty. Presley has the best attitude of anyone I have ever met. He has the unusual ability to find the good, the positive, and the hope in just about any situation or person. When I want to whine, complain, or belittle an issue or person, Presley refrains and instead offers encouragement and compliments. Even when he gets angry, which is rare, he comes back and gives the offender or situation a reprieve, a second chance.

Presley is the most positive, real person I know. I'm not talking about the fakes we have all met or know who gush, ha-ha, and ga-ga, then seem to crash or implode. I am not referring to folks who act one way in public and another way in private. My friend is the same whether he is in front of thousands or riding around at deer camp with a buddy. My opinion is that Presley's gift of having a positive, uplifting, and encouraging attitude is why he has been so successful. If I could learn only one trait from him, it would be his uncanny ability to always see the glass as half full. Because he has written this book, we can all learn so much more. I love you, brother!

—Randy Hedge
"The Cowboy"
De Queen, Arkansas

Introduction

The summers were always long and hot in Texas, but as a boy growing up in Pleasant Grove, I never seemed to notice. My childhood was full of the typical boyhood adventures—whether playing baseball at the Salvation Army or basketball at Pleasant Oaks Recreation Center—and I loved every second. It's a funny thing; as the innocence of youth fades away and the realities of your circumstances begin to set in, you realize just what life is like for you. As I started to get a little older, I began to figure out that Pleasant Grove was not that pleasant.

I grew up at 8724 Dunlap Drive. My mom took care of an elderly aunt, my grandmother, and me in an old 600-square-foot house. The street I grew up on had more drugs and violence than I care to remember. There were even two murders and a rape within seven houses of us.

My mom was the greatest mom a boy could ask for. I wouldn't trade my mom for ten mamas. She provided for us by working sixty hours a week in a sewing factory or school cafeteria. She taught me about life, love, and the Lord. I am the man I am today because of my mom. It was the saddest day of my life when she passed in 2008.

One thing my mom couldn't teach me about was finances. Mom grew up in the Depression era, during which just getting by was good enough. For some reason, I had a desire for more than just getting by. I found I had an increasing desire for me to be, do, and have more. This desire grew from an idea into a burning desire to succeed.

I was fortunate while growing up to have some fantastic role models through my participation in athletics: J.B. Kirk, Coach Henry Warren, Coach John Paul Fultz, and Coach J.D. Mayo. In sports, I began to learn valuable lessons about determination, leadership, and perseverance . . . lessons that became life-long principles by which I would live my life. School was, to me, a necessity to stay a member of the sports teams I had grown to love. Later, I realized that athletics was a key ingredient to keeping me out of the trouble that many adolescents find themselves in. When my friends would cross a line and ask me to join in, the risk of losing my place on the team proved far too great for me to go along.

After graduating from H. Grady Spruce High School, I enrolled at the University of Texas at Arlington. As I look back now, I realize I wasted a lot of my time at the university. I was in the "just get me out of here" program. Due to my love of athletics, as well as the many positive role models I found in my coaches, I decided to become a coach. I graduated from UTA with a degree in history, a minor in math, and a passion for coaching and leading others.

I was young and loved what I did, but life began to happen . . . fast! I woke up one day and found myself married, with two beautiful children, a mortgage, car payments, and the rest that life slams us with. I worked extra jobs after coaching and during the summers—painting, mowing yards, pouring concrete—anything I could do to help pay the bills. However, it was never enough. I found myself at the end of every month with more month than money. I used Visa to pay MasterCard and MasterCard to pay Discover. When something happened unexpectedly, like the need for new tires on the car, I found myself reworking four months of the budget just to get two new tires. I had arrived at a place I never thought I would be. I was living a life I never intended to live. I began to realize that the Lakers, Mavericks, and Celtics were not going to give me a call to coach their teams.

About this time, my cousins Tim and Diane Turley talked to me about a networking company. Like many people, I was skeptical but decided to take a look. I respected Tim and Diane and decided to join. I worked at it for a few months but decided it was not a company with which I wanted to be involved, and I began to search for something else to do. I looked in the classifieds at businesses for sale, franchise opportunities, and even new careers. The problem was that it cost a small fortune to start a business. I hardly had enough money to pay the bills! Somewhere along the way, I had failed to save the $1.5 million required for a McDonald's franchise. Seven years went by after my first exposure to networking, and I was in the exact same place financially. After sixteen years of coaching, several district titles, and numerous playoff appearances, I was only making $1,000 more per month than when I had started. I knew that if I wanted a change, I would have to make a change.

Jim Rohn, one of my all-time favorite personal development teachers, has a famous saying: "When the student is ready, a teacher will appear." I have found that it often works that way in my life, and God knew I was finally ready. My good friend and high school coach, J.D. Mayo, began talking to me about a new opportunity to get paid a residual income. It made a lot of sense to me; I was ready to make a change, so I joined his team.

I began carving out time to work my business, and I began experiencing success. Don't misunderstand . . . it was not "get rich quick" . . . it was a lot of hard work. But a journey had begun. Over the next few years, I created a residual income that gave me options. My time became my own. I was able to work when I wanted, how I wanted, and with whom I wanted. However, I had not accomplished my life-long dream of becoming financially free. What follows in these pages is the rest of the journey. You will hear about some of the thousands of friends I have made along the way. You will learn lessons from the actions I took that you can apply to your own journey. You will learn that it is not too late to become a millionaire by halftime.

CHAPTER 1 – Your Life Is the Big Leagues

A YOUNG BOY'S DREAM

It seems like only yesterday that my son Jordan was strapping on his first pair of baseball cleats, and I was buying him his first pack of baseball cards and watching him open the pack with such anticipation. I think back to the first major league baseball game I took him to, holding his hand as we found our way up the aisle to our seat. The noise of the crowd and the smell of nachos and popcorn . . . the effort was all worth it to see the look on his face as he watched his baseball heroes run onto the field! I also remember putting him in bed at night and finding his baseball glove tucked underneath his pillow. It was then that I realized my son was dreaming of playing in the major leagues!

Years later, in 2010, Jeanie and I got to see our son take that first step toward his dream when he was drafted in the second round of the 2010 Major League Baseball draft by the St. Louis Cardinals. Jordan is now working hard to make his dream of being in the big leagues come true.

ESCAPE FROM REALITY

Tonight, millions of Americans will huddle in front of their televisions to watch their favorite teams. We are mesmerized by our favorite athletes, captivated by their successes, worried about their health, and curious about their paychecks. We cheer for them. We want their autographs. We follow their tweets. We wear their jerseys.

On February 3, 2013, more than 76,000 fans piled inside the Mercedes-Benz Superdome in New Orleans for Super Bowl XLVII. The game had sold out almost immediately when the tickets went on sale, with an average ticket price of about $800. Another 108 million fans scheduled their lives around viewing the game from their televisions at home, at a friend's house, or at a sports bar. Many took off work. Many painted their faces. In addition, many lost their voices while screaming for their favorite team.

This seems so out of proportion to me! I can't fathom . . . 108 million people . . . all watching a football game! Now compare that number to the fact that only 13.5 million self-help books were sold the entire year of 2012. You would think more people would focus on improving their own lives, rather than spending their time and money watching other people live their lives.

Don't get me wrong, I'm a huge believer in sports! I coached for sixteen years, and my son is a professional athlete. As a basketball coach, I found sports to be extremely important. Sports teach our young people so many important things. But I also believe that we are losing our way as a society. We've lost touch with reality. And here is what most people miss: OUR OWN LIVES ARE THE REAL BIG LEAGUES.

The majority of people are looking to escape their reality by living vicariously through athletes or other celebrities. We've lost sight that our lives are the big leagues. Here in the real world, in the real big leagues, there are no do-overs.

WE ONLY GET ONE LIFE

The older I get, the more I appreciate every moment, every conversation, and every experience. The average life expectancy is seventy-eight years in this country. The average American has about 28,000 days to make his or her fortune and leave a mark, so for someone who is forty years old, that means you are at the halftime of life! You only have 1,981 Tuesdays left to create a legacy. Now, what if you or I only had $1,981 left in our bank account to spend? How would we use it? Would we waste it? I don't think so! We would spend every cent carefully! How much more so should we value our limited time? The Dalai Lama says, "To be born is a miracle. So what will you do with your life?" How profound!

We've all watched behind-the-scenes clips from our favorite Hollywood movies. We can hear the movie director yell, "Action!" and we cringe when they scream, "Cut!" when the scene isn't right. The fact is most movie scenes take three to four cuts to get it right.

But that's Hollywood . . . not real life. Outside movie studios, in this life, you and I only get one shot, one chance, and one opportunity. That's it. Yet I feel like so many people go through the day thinking that maybe they'll be given a second or third chance. They need to be reminded that in life there is no such thing as a dress rehearsal. This is it!

DREAMS CAN COME TRUE

Let's go back to my son Jordan and a young boy's dream of playing major league baseball. Many people will dismiss his story and chalk it up to good luck, inferring that their own dreams are dead or unattainable because they are not lucky. I disagree. The fact is, we all had dreams at one time in our life, and I believe that if you still have a heartbeat, deep down inside, you continue to have a dream!

I wrote this book to help you believe that we can all be, do, and have more! The pages of this book will serve as your guide. How do I know it works? Because I have done it! I was broke and facing foreclosure, with three hungry mouths to feed, not knowing what I could do. However, I believed. I believed there was a way. I found a mentor. I found an opportunity. I changed, I grew, and I took action! I did all the things I've outlined in this book, and I'm telling you that if you'll follow these principles and believe in yourself, you can achieve things beyond your wildest dreams!

When my journey in networking began, I had no idea Jeanie and I would earn $20 million in just eight years. When we started, we had no idea that we would be traveling the world, walking on beautiful beaches, and eating at the finest restaurants. We didn't know that we would have a chance to inspire thousands to achieve their dreams. We had no idea all this was in store for us.

We didn't know our future. Neither do you. With certainty, based on my own experience, the future is incredible for the person who is teachable, coachable, and willing to take action. If that's you, then it's time to begin!

WHERE TO BEGIN

It begins with the realization that our *lives* are the *real* big leagues, and from there, we must take full responsibility. The moment we take responsibility for every aspect of our life is the moment we start moving in the right direction.

Throughout this book, I mention bits and pieces of my childhood. My dad was an alcoholic who left us when I was nine years old. I grew up on the wrong side of the tracks, surrounded by drugs and violence. We were poor and struggled to make ends meet. These are all great-sounding excuses, but I finally realized that you can make excuses or you can make money, but you can't make both. My life started changing when I decided to take responsibility for my reality, when I made the decision that I wasn't going to let my past determine my future, when I realized there was no cavalry coming over the hill to save me. It was when I realized that if it was to be, it was up to me. When I realized my life was the big leagues, that's when things started changing.

WHO IS COUNTING ON YOU?

In 1940, bound from Liverpool to Canada, the *SS City of Benares* was sunk by a German U-boat, tossing the passengers into the ice-cold ocean waters in what would become one of the greatest stories of survival ever documented. Unfortunately, of the 407 passengers, a staggering 260 died waiting for rescue boats to arrive. What's interesting is that when the surviving passengers were interviewed days later, many of them said that what kept them from giving up was the thought of people back home who were counting on them. That single thought was enough fuel to endure the frigid waters long enough to be rescued. This is a remarkable example of how a strong "why" can empower us to overcome tremendous adversity.

I see myself on the playing field that I call "The Field of Life," and up in the grandstands sit my family. My wife is there. She is cheering for me. My daughter is there, too. She has painted my name on a banner and is holding it high in the air. My son is standing and screaming for his dad. I see them as my fans, supporting me and watching me. But it's more than that. They are also counting on me to deliver a win. They've put their faith and trust in me. I must come through. I don't see it as a choice. I see it as my duty.

You are in the big leagues, playing on your own field of life. Your grandstands are also full. All of your loved ones are there. They are waiting, watching, and wondering whether you'll win. So will you? Will you win? Will you do what it takes? Will you pay the price? Will you fight for them? I know who is counting on me. The question is, who is counting on you?

HOMEWORK

As a coach, sometimes I would give my players homework. Here is yours.

1. Grab a sheet of paper and complete this powerful exercise. Simply write down the names of three people who are counting on you to succeed in your networking business.

2. Under each name, be descriptive and write about how your success will change his or her life. Write a descriptive scene in the future with this person celebrating your success. Include the sights and sounds, and write about how you will feel.

3. Keep doing this exercise any time you face adversity in your business. This exercise will refocus your mind and give you strength to keep going, to survive, and ultimately to achieve your goals!

CHAPTER 2 – The Network Marketing Profession

"Network marketing gives people the opportunity, with very low risk and very low financial commitment, to build their own income-generating asset and acquire great wealth."

—ROBERT T. KIYOSAKI

THE CHANGING TIMES

A generation or two ago, the best path to financial success was to go to college, make good grades, get a job with a sound company, and work hard for that company for thirty or forty years. Everything has changed. Today, companies are downsizing, going virtual, or outsourcing to other countries. This change has fostered a much stronger interest in home-based businesses. People want to control their own future, and for most, it's not good enough to just scratch out a living anymore. Everyone wants the best this life has to offer. Nobody enjoys living in mediocrity and feeling second class. People want to live with passion and have a lifestyle.

So, how do you end up where you would like to be? What you are about to see is simply a vehicle that can take you from where you are now to where you would like to go. It's a vehicle to help you own your own business, have the convenience of working from home, enjoy financial security, experience the comfort of stress-free living, and realize the prestige of being successful and making lots of money. This potential is the result of network marketing. As you get involved and start to understand the power of network marketing, you will start to learn the power of leverage and residual income.

As J. Paul Getty put it, "I would rather have one percent of the efforts of a hundred people than one hundred percent of my own efforts." Getty was talking about leverage and residual income. Residual income is doing something once and continuing to be paid for it over and over again. Residual income keeps coming in long after the work is finished. Best-selling authors, hit songwriters, and investors enjoy residual income, while common folks like us have historically been left out in the dark. That is, until network marketing came along. Networking has opened the door to financial freedom for everyone.

LEVERAGE AND TWELVE-YEAR-OLD WARREN BUFFETT

If you're like me, you might have thought that Warren Buffett was born wise and rich, trading stocks from his crib. The fact is, Warren Buffett started from the bottom and rose to the top by using this idea: leverage. Here is how it started . . . when Warren was nine years old, his father put him to work during his summer break at his grandfather's grocery store. From there, he went on to selling stamps, recycling bottles, and washing cars. By the age of 12, he had progressed to having his own paper route and owning a lawn business that serviced his neighborhood.

At the end of every summer, as soon as school started, Warren's mother wanted her young son fully focused on his academics. For Warren, this meant no more business, no more selling, and no more making money until the following summer. Warren asked himself a very simple question: "How can I make money while I stay focused on my academics?" The answer came to him in the form of a gumball machine. He could buy a gumball machine, and while he was in school, his gumball machine could be making him money!

At the young age of twelve, Warren took his summer money, bought a gumball machine, and placed it in the local barbershop. From there, he took his gumball profits and invested in a used pinball machine. One pinball machine led to two. Two machines led to three. Before long, he had many pinball machines all around town! Warren Buffett had figured out leverage.

LEVERAGE IN NETWORK MARKETING

It's our turn to learn about leverage. There are only so many hours in a week. With a JOB (acronym for Just Over Broke), we can only trade so much time for so much money. Let's say you are a workaholic and you work sixty hours a week. Assuming four weeks in a month, that's 240 hours per month.

Now, let's contrast that with building a network marketing team. Let's say you sponsor three, who sponsor three, who sponsor three, who sponsor three. You are down four levels (3-9-27-81) and have a team of 120 associates. Let's assume those 120 associates average just four hours a week working on their new business. That's 120 associates working four hours a week for four weeks. That's (120 x 4 x 4) 1,920 hours a month. Would you rather have 240 hours of your labor or 1,920 hours of the team's labor? I will take the team. As you start to experience what it's like to leverage time and create passive residual income, you will have a new appreciation for the amazing power of leverage . . . just as Warren Buffett did.

COACH'S SUCCESS TIP:

CREATING LEVERAGE CAN CHANGE YOUR LIFE.

A LOOK AT NETWORK MARKETING

Networking has been around for decades, and the idea behind networking is simple. Instead of spending millions of dollars advertising to promote products or services, companies pay common people for the best form of advertising there is: word of mouth. A friend telling a friend yields results unmatched in traditional advertising. Instead of companies paying celebrity spokespeople, they pay us. Businesses love the no-risk advertising word of mouth provides, and associates love getting a piece of the advertising pie for doing something they have been doing their whole lives for free—talking.

The famous merchant John Wanamaker once said, "Half the money I spend on advertising is wasted. The problem is, I don't know which half." Such is the dilemma with all traditional advertising. Just look around at all the money spent on advertising products and services:

Telemarketing	Door hangers	Radio
Newspapers	Television	Magazines
Door to door	Direct mail	Billboards

The total amount spent by traditional companies on advertising products and services each year comes to billions of dollars. However, none of these advertising methods is as effective as word of mouth—network marketing. Potential customers will give more credence to a friend's recommendation than to a recommendation from a celebrity spokesperson on television. Through networking, we can get our piece of this enormous pie.

Almost every product and service is now being offered through network marketing: energy, telephone service, legal services, insurance, buyer discount services, makeup, vitamins, coffee, travel services, water filters, home products, greeting cards . . . and the list goes on and on.

Today, networking has emerged as the new paradigm of personal and business development. It is recognized as one of the fastest-growing business models in the world. It is estimated that there are more than 50 million people involved in network marketing worldwide, with more than $165 billion in annual revenue.

The success of networking has been written about in every business publication available, including *Forbes, Newsweek, The Wall Street Journal, Fortune, Time, Success, USA Today*, and more. Billionaires such as Warren Buffett, Kenny Troutt, Richard Branson, and Donald Trump have owned or currently own network marketing companies. Distinguished economist and best-selling author Paul Zane Pilzer sees network marketing as the base for America's next big boom. He predicts that millions of new millionaires will be created in the next few years through networking.

BE AN ENTREPRENEUR

Working for someone else or toiling in someone else's field makes their dreams come true, not yours. As long as you work for someone else, chances are you won't make life-changing income. Ninety-plus percent of the wealthy became wealthy by owning their own businesses. They created wealth by earning profits, not working for wages.

The industrialist Cornelius Vanderbilt created wealth by following his personal motto: "Never be a minion; always be an owner." Network marketing teaches us how to make that transition: from minion to owner, from employee to entrepreneur! It teaches people how to build global businesses out of their homes. When you own your own business, you write your own history, you write your own success story, you write your own legacy and, most importantly, you write your own paycheck. Network marketing is the most awesome phenomenon in the history of American capitalism. Not everyone can be a pro baseball player, a professional singer, a movie star, or a brain surgeon. However, anyone with a reasonable amount of intelligence can excel at networking.

Network marketing attracts men and women of all ages, backgrounds, and socioeconomic groups. Success in networking doesn't require specialized skills or sales training. Associates from all walks of life can build huge teams. Some associates are successful, highly educated professionals while others are from the wrong side of the tracks. Associates may have little education, no business background, and no sales experience. Networking is more about heart and how much you want to change your life. It's more about action than ability. It's about honesty, integrity, and hard work. In other words, you can be a common person with a burning desire to be somebody, and you can achieve amazing success.

COACH'S SUCCESS TIP:

YOU MUST WORK FOR YOURSELF IF YOU WANT TO ACHIEVE FINANCIAL INDEPENDENCE.

STOP TRADING TIME FOR MONEY

If you are willing to focus and work hard for two to five years, you have a chance to make a six-figure monthly income and achieve financial and time freedom. In what other business can a blue-collar worker make more in a month than a successful professional earns in a year? Whether you are a store clerk earning minimum wage or a world-renowned surgeon, you have one thing in common: you are trading time for money. This is linear income. The day you stop working is the day you stop being paid. Trading time for money won't result in financial and time freedom. However, residual income created through network marketing can.

As a personal example of what leverage can do, some weeks I work and some weeks I don't. Let's take a look at how residual income works. Last week, I probably worked about ten hours and made about $60,000. Next week, I think I will go to West Palm Beach and watch Jordan play baseball. But the money will come in again. It's a great feeling knowing that money is coming in whether I work or not. Some weeks I don't work any, and my income goes up. Financial freedom is created through the leverage that network marketing gives us. My buddy and one of the world's best networkers, Randy Hedge says, "It's not about what you do, but about what you start." With linear income, you work once and are paid once. If you stop working, you stop being paid. With leverage, you are paid repeatedly for working once.

Leverage is awesome; unfortunately, it's not taught in school. Most people don't have a clue what leverage is. If you have a good understanding of leverage and apply it, it can change your life. What would your life be like if you had money coming into your account that had little or nothing to do with your working? Money that comes in week after week, month after month, and year after year? Passive, residual income that allows you to have the freedom to live your life the way you want to live it, buy what you want to buy, live where you want to live, and drive what you want to drive? Isn't it time that you start making the transition from your linear income job to passive residual income created by leverage through your network marketing business?

COACH'S SUCCESS TIP:

RESIDUAL INCOME CREATED THROUGH NETWORK MARKETING CAN CREATE FINANCIAL AND TIME FREEDOM.

EASE OF ENTRY

A huge advantage to networking over traditional business is the ease of entry. Network marketing is a low-investment, low-overhead business in which common people can achieve amazing results. It doesn't take a huge capital investment to get started. For a small entry fee, the company provides the tools, training, and support systems to get individuals started in their businesses.

PICK A COMPANY

Now that you know a little about networking, it's time to pick a company that will share its advertising budget with you. Join a company that offers a product or service that people need and/or want – a company that you feel comfortable with and that you believe in.

There are many great network marketing companies. The potential is real. There are millions of dollars to be made, and compared to traditional business models, this can be accomplished relatively quickly.

In a nutshell, my advice about getting started is to do your research, pick a good company, and then put in a small amount of money, a lot of hard work, and a great deal of perseverance. Success will not happen overnight, but if you stick with it, you will find what you seek.

HOMEWORK

1. Think of the wealthiest person you know *outside* network marketing. How has he or she used the concept of leverage to create a fortune?

2. Reach out to three people in the top-ranked position of your chosen network marketing company, and ask them to share their story about how network marketing has changed their lives. Be sure to share those stories with as many prospects and teammates as you possibly can!

3. Follow or join the Facebook pages and Twitter feeds for the three people you identified in step 2.

CHAPTER 3 – If You Want More, You Must Become More

"Formal education will make you a living. Self-education will make you a fortune."

—Jim Rohn

In 2002, a small-town garbage man by the name of Michael Fritter won a $15 million lottery jackpot. He was an overnight financial success who became a local legend and a small-town hero: "Garbage Man Now Multimillionaire!" However, eight years later, Michael Fritter was back in front of his old boss, penniless, asking for his garbage collection job back. Why?

Similarly, William Post thought his problems were over when he won the 1988 Pennsylvania lottery, a whopping $16.2 million prize! However, when he died in 2006, he was broke, living off a measly $450-per-month disability check. Why?

Stories like this seem all too common: people suddenly experience a windfall of money only to wind up broke . . . or worse. In the NFL, where the average salary is $770,000 per year, reports show us that 78 percent of all NFL players find themselves bankrupt or in severe financial distress within two years of retiring. Why?

Here's why: Your income will match the person who you are. I now firmly believe that to have more, you must first become more. People don't make what they want . . . they make what they are.

CHANGE IS WITHIN YOUR CONTROL

For all of us, whether we're an NFL player or a network marketer, there is no avoiding this cold, hard fact: your income is ultimately determined by the person you are. However, the wonderful news is that you can change. Change is something within each of our control.

Once again, network marketing plays a key role. Your network marketing company provides you with the perfect environment to help you grow. Many refer to network marketing as a personal growth course with a compensation plan attached. This is true. It's a journey toward becoming the person you know deep down inside you can become!

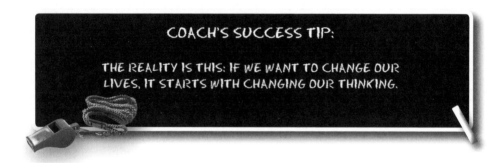

COACH'S SUCCESS TIP:

THE REALITY IS THIS: IF WE WANT TO CHANGE OUR LIVES, IT STARTS WITH CHANGING OUR THINKING.

CHANGE YOUR THINKING, CHANGE YOUR LIFE

From the time we were in our mama's arms, we were being conditioned on how we think about things. Our parents were modeling for us. Our grandparents were modeling for us. Siblings, friends of the family, and everyone with whom we spent time influenced our thinking and actions. We were watching what everyone was doing and listening to what everyone was saying. We were becoming conditioned.

I had the best mom in the world. She was the most loving, Godly woman I have ever known. My mom was awesome. She taught me about life, love, friends, and the Lord. I am the man I am today because of my mom. However, as I touched on in the introduction, my mom grew up in the

Depression, where just getting by was good enough. Therefore, I was conditioned to just get by. Mom didn't do that on purpose. She wanted the best for me; she just didn't know any differently. I had to change. I had to reprogram.

The vast majority of people have no idea how their beliefs got into their heads, and most of us have had our beliefs for so long that we don't even notice them anymore. Our thoughts are so ingrained that they have become automatic. Our minds are set, and unless something rocks our boat, we see no need to examine our thoughts and beliefs.

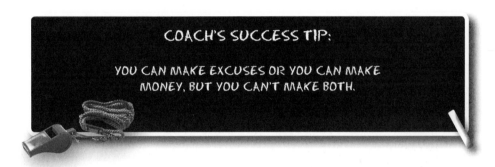

COACH'S SUCCESS TIP:

YOU CAN MAKE EXCUSES OR YOU CAN MAKE MONEY, BUT YOU CAN'T MAKE BOTH.

DO IT TWICE

Anything of significance that we do in life must be done twice. The first place is in our mind. If we think we can . . . we can. If we think we can't . . . we can't. When you believe . . . really believe something can be done . . . your mind goes to work to help you find a way to do it. I've found some of the most practical success-building wisdom is found in the Biblical statement that faith can move mountains. Believe you can move a mountain, and you can. You must believe in what you are doing if you want to accomplish great and mighty things.

BE A LIFE-LONG LEARNER

On January 6, 1919, former President Theodore Roosevelt died at home in his sleep. Then–Vice President Marshall said, "Death had to take him sleeping, for if Roosevelt had been awake, there would have been a fight." When they took him from his bed, they found a book under his pillow. Theodore Roosevelt, whose list of accomplishments is remarkable, was still striving to learn and improve himself up to the very end. He was truly a life-long learner.

A good friend of mine, Gerald Brooks, introduced me to John C. Maxwell. Maxwell is arguably the foremost authority on leadership alive today. I was invited to fly to San Diego and spend some time with John. It was a great pleasure meeting John, and we had an awesome time getting to know each other. We had a lot in common. He loves the Lord, basketball, and networking. Many things from that first introduction stay with me, but something John said is especially appropriate here. He said, "Most people want their lives to keep improving, yet they value peace and stability at the same time. People often forget that you can't improve and still stay the same. Growth means change. Change requires challenging the status quo. If you want greater possibilities, you can't settle for what you have now."

MIND FOOD

To grow, it's imperative that we read good books, listen to quality audio, attend seminars, and run with winners. The simple truth is that how you feed your mind is every bit as critical to your success as how you feed your body. The body is what the body is fed and, by the same token, the mind is what the mind is fed. Mind food doesn't come in nice, neat little packages that you buy at the grocery store. Mind food is your environment. It's how you are conditioned. It's all the people with whom you spend time. It's all the television shows you watch. It's all the books you read. It's all the countless things that influence your conscious and subconscious thoughts. What we put in our mind determines our attitudes, habits, personality, and, ultimately, our level of success. Be environmentally conscious. Don't let negative forces enter your mind. Don't let small thinkers hold you back. Put good stuff in your mind, and spend time with successful people. Let's talk about each one individually.

READ GOOD BOOKS

Winners are readers who pay close attention to what they read. I suggest you read inspirational autobiographies of successful people. Read books on personal growth, psychology, sales, finance, and health. Study the principles of successful living. Read books that are positive and uplifting—and that teach you something worthwhile. Read from authors like John C. Maxwell, Zig Ziglar, Napoleon Hill, Stephen Covey, and T. Harv Eker. The list of authors who have written books aimed at personal growth is endless. See my Game Plan Reading List at the end of this book.

Share what you're reading for inspiration on your Twitter feed and Facebook wall (using #CoachPresley) and let others know what books are helping you!

READING ACTION STEP

If you read ten pages from a good book today, will it change your life? No, chances are it won't. But if you read ten pages today and again tomorrow and again the next day and the next day and the next day, over the course of a year, you will have read 3,650 pages—the equivalent of one or two dozen books of life-transforming material! Will your life change after reading dozens of good books? Absolutely! We can all find ten to fifteen minutes to read ten pages a day if we are serious about changing our lives. Let's make the commitment to start reading today!

LISTEN TO QUALITY AUDIO

Use your rolling university. The average American spends about thirty minutes commuting each day. In five years, that's 1,250 hours in the car—enough time to give you the equivalent of a four-year college education! Spend that time listening to quality audio that will change your life instead of tuning into negative news. Audio books and audio programs can teach you how to be successful in all areas of your life. If you are ready to grow as a person, make a commitment to use the time in your car for education and not entertainment.

ATTEND SEMINARS

In addition to reading good books and listening to quality audio, attend seminars designed to help you change your life. By attending these seminars, you learn from many of the greatest speakers, trainers, and motivators of our day. Additionally, you benefit from the excitement and inspiration of your fellow attendees and the networking that goes on at these events. I have had the pleasure of attending many seminars and listening to many great speakers, and the results have been astounding. I'm not the same person because of what I've learned at these events.

Robert Kiyosaki, author of the best-selling book, *Rich Dad, Poor Dad*, said, "I go to seminars. I like it when they are at least two days long, because I like to immerse myself in a subject. In 1973, I was watching TV and this guy came on advertising a three-day seminar on how to buy real estate for nothing down . . . that course has made me at least $2 million, if not more. Most importantly, it bought me my life. I don't have to work for the rest of my life because of that one course. I go to at least two such courses every year." Find a seminar that interests you . . . and get started learning.

> *"Don't join an easy crowd. Go where the expectations and the demands to perform are high."*
>
> —JIM ROHN

RELATIONSHIPS

Relationships in our lives really do make us or break us. They add or subtract. They give us energy or they take it away. They lift us up or they pull us down. Here are a couple of ways to determine whether a relationship is positive or negative. The first is to ask whether a person makes you feel better or worse about yourself. The second is to evaluate how much energy the relationship requires. Let's face it, some relationships feel like they are sucking the life right out of us. I would dare say these relationships involve negative people.

I have a theory on negative people: "You are negative . . . my legs still work . . . I'm out of here!" In the long run, a negative relationship cannot influence you in a positive direction. Your future is too important to risk associating with negative people who are living failures. Your relationships will define you, so choose your friends wisely. If you can't change the people around you, then change the people you're around!

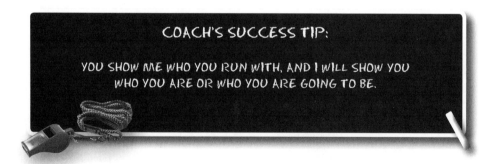

COACH'S SUCCESS TIP:

YOU SHOW ME WHO YOU RUN WITH, AND I WILL SHOW YOU WHO YOU ARE OR WHO YOU ARE GOING TO BE.

TEAM MEETING

When I was coaching at Lakeview High School, I always held a meeting with my team at the beginning of the year. At this meeting, I covered many topics.

I talked about how I wanted them to act and dress. I discussed the importance of good conduct and grades. And there was one statement I always made at some point during this meeting: "You show me who you run with, and I will show you who you are or who you are going to be." I wanted my players to stay on the right path, be productive students, and stay out of trouble. I knew that whom they ran with greatly influenced their success or failure.

While I'm not worried about your getting in trouble at school, I make the same statement to you that I made to my players: "You show me who you run with, and I will show you who you are or who you are going to be." If you want to accomplish great things with your life, you must hang with people who have what you want or who are at least pulling the rope the same way you are pulling it. If you are running with positive, motivated people who see the glass as half full, it will rub off on you. You will start seeing all the possibilities for your life. But the flip side is also true. If you are hanging with negative, dull, disillusioned, frustrated crybabies, you are swimming against the current, and you are going to find it tough to break out. There is a saying: "Inmates don't like to see another prisoner escape."

Be careful whom you run with, because it's a fact that you begin to think like the people you spend a lot of time with. Each relationship in your life has either a positive or a negative impact on you. Surround yourself with positive, motivated people. If you want to be successful, you need to run with successful people.

YOUR FIVE BEST FRIENDS

Your income tends to equal the average of the incomes of your five best friends, and this principle doesn't only apply to your finances—it applies to every aspect of your life. Your personal growth will be about the average level of the personal growth of your five closest friends. Your health will be about the average level of the health of your five closest friends. Your finances, health, success, relationships, and everything else in your life will be very close to the average level of your five best friends. We have all heard the phrases, "Birds of a feather flock together," "You are known by the company you keep," and, "Show me where you fish, and I will show you what you catch." They are all true.

If your five best friends are negative, it's next to impossible for you to be positive. If your five closest friends are living in the past, always complaining, blaming others for their lack of success, and always acting negatively, then the odds of your being successful are slim. If you are around negative people all the time, it is highly unlikely that you will be positive. Remember, people who tell you that it can't be done are usually unsuccessful. They are, at best, average in terms of accomplishments. Develop a defense against people who want to convince you that you can't do it. If you want to be successful, you need to have relationships with successful people.

COACH'S SUCCESS TIP:

SURROUND YOURSELF WITH WINNERS.

FIND A COACH

We can all use a little coaching, so find a mentor. Look for a mentor who has become successful through his or her own achievements and hard work. Find someone who has accomplished amazing things in life because he or she had extraordinary discipline and refused to be denied. This person was relentless in the pursuit of dreams and goals. You are looking for a mentor who has traits that you admire and who inspires you to set the bar higher.

I have a strong group of mentors in my life, and I make sure to spend quality time with them each month. When I leave my mentors, I feel energized and full of ideas, and I usually see things differently. My mentors are truly indispensable to my success and my life.

Throughout our lifetime, we are in contact with thousands of people. Most have a very limited impact on us, but there are a few relationships that have a tremendous impact on us and change the course of our lives. These relationships are pivotal to who we are and what we accomplish.

I have a story that certainly illustrates how one of my mentors influenced my life in a major way. I had a cousin who lived in the same part of town that I did—the wrong side of the tracks. He was my first cousin, my mom's brother's son, Manny Carter.

THE STORY OF MANNY CARTER

Manny was a few years older than I was but grew up poor as I did. As a kid, I can remember watching Manny as he worked odd jobs, mowed yards, and threw a paper route. Manny did all kinds of stuff to make a few bucks. A lot of us did odd jobs, but the thing that was different about Manny was that he always saved some of his money.

Most of our family didn't go to high school, but Manny graduated from W.W. Samuell High School and then did what no one else in our family had done: he went to college at the University of Texas. Starting with the money he had saved from his odd jobs, he worked himself through UT and graduated.

After graduation, Manny got a job with Mobil Oil Company, before Mobil merged with Exxon. As Manny worked his way up the ladder at Mobil, where he eventually became a vice president, Manny would buy a piece of real estate, invest in a company, and play the stock market . . . things that up until that time were foreign to me. Today, because of his hard work and investments, Manny is worth a few million dollars.

I remember being a kid and loving to spend time with Manny. I liked to go over to Manny's house because he lived in a big, beautiful home in a nice neighborhood and had new BMWs in the driveway. At Christmas, Manny's house was decorated immaculately with lots of presents under the tree and lots of food to eat. I stayed over at Manny's as much as I could; I just didn't want to leave. I vividly remember one evening, walking from Manny's house and getting into my old, beat-up Ford Galaxy to head back to 8724 Dunlap Drive (where people were getting raped and murdered) thinking, "I want to be like Manny! Manny is who I want to be like!"

Until just a few years ago, Manny never knew what an influence he had on my life. He was my role model, and he didn't even know it. I wasn't one of his kids; I was a cousin a few years younger, but I realized that if Manny could do it, I could do it. Manny was from the same family as I. Manny was from the same part of town as I. Manny had grown up as I did. It just kept going through my mind that if Manny could do it, I could do it! I'm writing this book today because a man named Manny Carter stood in the gap for our family and showed us that we could break the pattern and be successful. My question to you is this: what legacy are you leaving for your family?

HOMEWORK

1. Start reading at least ten pages a day from a good book.

2. Listen to audiobooks and programs when you are driving in your rolling university.

3. Attend at least two seminars each year.

4. Examine the people in your life. Are they positive influences or negative influences? Are they pulling you up or dragging you down? Write down the ten people with whom you associate the most, and ask yourself these three questions:

    i. Is this someone I should STOP associating with?

    ii. Is this someone I should LIMIT my association with?

    iii. Is this someone I should EXPAND my association with?

5. Find a mentor.

CHAPTER 4 – Get Out of Your Comfort Zone

"Move out of your comfort zone. You can only grow if you are willing to feel awkward and uncomfortable when you try something new."

—Brian Tracy

BROADEN YOUR HORIZONS

This may sound crazy, but writing this book took me way out of my comfort zone. I have always loved numbers, but struggled in English. Jeanie will tell you that grammar and spelling are not my strong suits. And here I was, thinking about writing a book! Are we talking about the same guy who could barely spell "author?"

The thought of writing a book scared me to death. However, as I started to put some thoughts down on paper, the fear began to fade. As I started formulating the chapters, it occurred to me, "I can do this." The more I worked on the book, the bigger my comfort zone grew. Writing this book was another confirmation to me that we must tackle our fears head on.

Getting out of our comfort zone is tough. Understandably, many associates would like to grow a huge, successful network marketing organization without getting out of their comfort zones. Unfortunately, that simply is not possible.

If you want to do great things in your life, you must push yourself. When I started networking, I hated picking up the phone to set appointments. I was a coach. I taught people how to shoot a basketball . . . I didn't set appointments. I would literally get sick to my stomach when it was time to make the calls, but I realized that to grow my business and change my life, I had to do it. It was kind of like writing this book in that the more I did it, the easier it became. Today, I can pick up the phone and call anyone, and it no longer bothers me. My comfort zone grew and so can yours.

HAVE COURAGE

I will never tell you that getting out of your comfort zone is easy, but I will tell you that it's worth it. We must have courage as we build our network marketing businesses. We must understand that courage is not the absence of fear; rather, it is the judgment that something else is more important than fear. Courage is being afraid and doing it anyway. I have also learned that courage does not always roar . . . sometimes courage is the quiet voice at the end of the day that says, "I will try again tomorrow."

I have never seen anything great accomplished in life without effort, without pain, and without commitment. Nature demonstrates this all the time. Rose bushes have to be pruned to reach full blossom, diamonds are formed only through intense pressure, and the hottest fires produce the hardest steel. Remember, it is not easy to expand your comfort zone, but it is worth the effort.

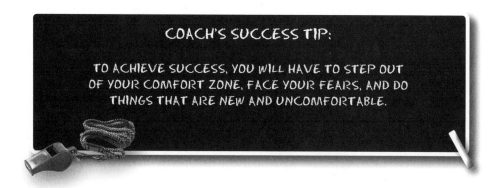

COACH'S SUCCESS TIP:

TO ACHIEVE SUCCESS, YOU WILL HAVE TO STEP OUT OF YOUR COMFORT ZONE, FACE YOUR FEARS, AND DO THINGS THAT ARE NEW AND UNCOMFORTABLE.

MOMENTS OF DECISION

Moments of decision make us who we are. We all experience these moments every day. From the time we wake up until we go to bed, we face decisions: Do I get out of bed, or do I hit the snooze? Do I watch TV, or do I read a good book? Do I make the call, or do I let fear stop me? Do I bring up my new business, or do I keep my mouth shut? In reality, these are the moments when we're on the edge of our comfort zone. Do we pull back? Or do we expand?

Jeanie and I have made millions of dollars in network marketing, and even with all the success, I still face the same daily moments of decision that everyone else does. In fact, I've come to realize that everyone has these moments of fear. Everyone is tempted to do what's convenient, to pull back, to settle. But winners never settle! Winners understand that it's these moments—when they come face-to-face with the cliff of their own comfort zone—that can give them separation from their competition.

WHAT IS A WINNER?

Winners live and breathe success. Winners don't let pessimism dictate. Winners don't believe in giving in to negative forces. Winners get out of their comfort zones. Winners are the happiest individuals because they accomplish more with their lives. Winners find life rewarding, exciting, and worthwhile. Winners look forward to each new day and each new challenge. Winners simply have a different attitude . . . a winning attitude.

WHAT IS A WINNING ATTITUDE?

A winning attitude is a personal decision to believe you can accomplish great and mighty things in your life. A winning attitude is more important than ability for success in networking. In other words, it is attitude and not aptitude that ultimately determines your altitude. It is a mental leap of faith whereby you believe that each day's events will validate your expectation of good results. Maintaining a winning attitude is not easy. It demands lots of work and continually high vigilance. You will have to focus on it every day, but there are few, if any, things in life that will pay bigger dividends than a winning attitude. A person's attitude transcends every part of his or her life. If you look at the mental and physical traits that humans possess, attitude stands at the top of the list as the great divide between average performance and

33

peak achievement. A winning attitude is based on faith that life is inherently awesome and belief that, with perseverance, you will ultimately reach your dreams. You must have the attitude that winning is not optional.

WINNER VS. LOSERS

1. Winners believe they create their life; losers believe life happens to them.
2. Winners think big; losers think small.
3. Winners focus on opportunity; losers focus on obstacles.
4. Winners admire rich and successful people; losers resent rich and successful people.
5. Winners play the money game to win; losers play the money game not to lose.
6. Winners associate with positive, successful people; losers associate with negative people.
7. Winners manage their money well; losers mismanage their money.
8. Winners are bigger than their problems; losers are smaller than their problems.
9. Winners choose to get paid based on results; losers choose to get paid based on time.
10. Winners act in spite of fear; losers let fear stop them.
11. Winners have their money work hard for them; losers work hard for their money.
12. Winners constantly learn and grow; losers think they know it all.

DERRICK ROSE AND DAVID COPPERFIELD

Adidas recently did a special interview with Chicago Bulls superstar Derrick Rose. In the interview, Rose says, "The moment I'm tired and ready to quit practicing, I realize that it's those moments that everyone else quits. Therefore, if I keep going, I know I can separate myself from my competition. So I keep going." In similar fashion, world-famous magician David Copperfield, in an interview on *Oprah*, said, "People mistakenly think I have no fears. No, of course I have fears. I just decide to charge at them head-on!"

The word crisis literally means "point of decision." Every day when you come face-to-face with the edge of your comfort zone, you're at a moment of crisis, a point of decision. And it's a decision with only two options. Either you advance, or you stay the same. It's that simple. I'm asking you to advance, to attack, and to charge your fears head on!

WHAT IS HARD CAN BECOME EASY

Remember the first time you tried to tie your own shoes? It seemed hard, impossible almost. You struggled. It was tedious. It was annoying. But you did it because you wanted to be a big boy or a big girl, and over time, it became easier and easier. It became so easy, in fact, that if you think back to this morning, it's likely you tied your shoes without even thinking about it.

Everything that's hard can become easy if we continue to do it. Repetition is the key. I've put this chapter on comfort zone in the book to encourage you because what seems hard now will become easy if we tackle it head on. In other words, what's outside your comfort zone now can one day be inside your comfort zone. You'll actually look back and laugh, saying, "I can't believe I used to be scared of that."

THE REAL SECRET TO ESCAPING YOUR COMFORT ZONE

In the Hollywood film *Castaway*, Tom Hanks's character is marooned on a small, deserted island. Feeling alone and forgotten, he faces the realization that there is no search party looking for him, that friends and family have given up on his being alive, believing him to be dead at sea. With no visible hope of escape, this island slowly becomes his new comfort zone. Ultimately, for him to have a chance to get off the island, he has to overcome his fear and launch out to sea on a flimsy, hand-made vessel.

Did you ever stop to think about what caused this character to overcome his fear to leave the island (his comfort zone) to attack the sea and launch into the unknown with no guarantee of survival? What inspired him? Well, if you saw the film, you will remember that every night before he closed his eyes to go to sleep, he would gaze at a small weathered photo of his sweetheart, the love of his life back home. The thought of her was enough to inspire his brave escape of the island.

What's my point here? There's a secret to escaping your comfort zone, and it's woven into this movie. The secret is this: You must keep focused on your dream. When your vision is clear, you will pay the price!

If you have a dream and you are excited about where you are going, you'll pay the price. You'll do what it takes. Tom Hanks's character looked at that photo every night. He stayed focused on his dream. We need to do the same. When we're focused on our dream, we'll gladly pay any price, even if it means getting out of our comfort zones!

THE COMFORT ZONE

I used to have a comfort zone,
Where I knew I couldn't fail.
The same four walls and busy work
Were really more like jail.
I longed so much to do the things
I'd never done before . . .
But I stayed inside my comfort zone
And paced the same old floor.
I said it didn't matter that
I wasn't doing much.
I said I didn't care for things
Like boats and cars and such.
I claimed to be so busy
With things inside "my zone,"
But deep inside I longed for something
Special of my own.
I couldn't let my life go by
Just watching others win . . .
So I held my breath and took a step
To let the change begin!
I took that step and with new strength
I'd never felt before,
I kissed my comfort zone good-bye,
And closed and locked the door!
If you are in your COMFORT ZONE,
Afraid to venture out . . .
Remember that all winners were
At one time filled with doubt!
A step or two and words of praise
Can make your dreams come true.
So—greet your future with a smile . . .
SUCCESS IS THERE FOR YOU!

—Unknown

HOMEWORK

1. Grab a pen and paper. Write down a recent moment of decision in your networking business when you faced a decision but backed off because it was outside your comfort zone. How will you react differently next time?

2. Close your eyes. See yourself as someone who attacks fear head on. See yourself in different situations acting boldly, as you know you can. Remember, for things to happen in reality, they must first happen in your mind.

3. On your refrigerator, bathroom mirror, and car visor, put pictures that remind you of your dreams. Look at these pictures every morning and every night. Anytime you feel down, revisit your dream. Feel what it will be like to have your dreams become a reality.

4. Upload a picture of one of your dreams to your Facebook wall. Add a description to explain your dream, and ask your followers to post their dreams to their pages, too! Make sure to also post them to my Facebook wall www.facebook.com/presleyswagerty.

CHAPTER 5 – Dream Big. No, Bigger!

"The future belongs to those who believe in the beauty of their dreams."

—Napoleon Hill

STORY OF THE TWO BOYS IN THE WOODS

Two best friends, both nine years old, were playing in the woods. It was winter, and snow covered the ground. They came to a small pond surrounded by trees and frozen over by the cold. Not thinking, the boys wandered onto the ice as they played. All of a sudden, one of the boys fell through the ice and plunged into the freezing water.

His friend ran over to the bank in desperation, looking for help. He couldn't find anything so he climbed the nearest tree and reached for the longest branch. Grabbing the branch, the little boy ripped the branch from the trunk and dragged it across the ice. With all his strength, he extended the branch to his friend and pulled him to safety. He had saved his buddy's life!

When locals heard of the nine-year-old hero and how this little boy ripped a huge branch from the trunk of a tree, they couldn't believe it. "It's not possible," the townspeople claimed. "There's no way a little boy could do such a thing."

Overhearing the conversation, a wise old man spoke up, "I know how he was able to do it."

"How?" the townspeople wanted to know. Calmly, the old man said, "He could do it because no one was around to tell him that he couldn't!"

YOU'VE BEEN CONDITIONED

Wow! That story gives me goose bumps. It reminds me of how we live in a world in which we've been conditioned to settle and to be ordinary. It seems we live in a society that mocks the dreamers and finds enjoyment in their failures. If you dream about being something great, it seems to threaten those around you; it's as if you're indirectly saying you want to leave them somehow, and they don't want you to leave, or dream, or succeed. Misery loves company. Many events and people around you may be conditioning you to be ordinary . . . don't listen!

THE DREAM INSIDE YOU

In Tim Burton's film *Big Fish*, the main character, Edward Bloom, decided to leave Ashton, Alabama, saying, "This town is too small for a man of my ambition." Do you ever feel like that? Do you feel as though your ambition has outgrown your surroundings? Do you feel that the life you're living is not the one you were intended to live? Do you feel you were meant for something more? Is there something burning inside that's telling you that you can be, do, and have more? I ask because some people seem to be content with living small lives of mediocrity. They make excuses why life didn't work out for them. Robin Sharma says, "Potential unexpressed leads to pain."

But that is not me! And by picking up this book, I know that's not you, either. You have a dream. You have something inside you: Potential begging for expression. You refuse to live small, and you have a dream for what life should be like. So take heart. Understand your dream is possible. It is achievable. You can be, do, and have anything you want in this life!

DREAMS

In my experience, the most rewarding way to experience life is by passionately pursuing your dreams. Work hard to bring into focus your ideal vision for your dream life, because that is when you are the most alive. Wake up each morning expecting great things to happen. If you have never had that feeling, then get to work on your dreams. When you have a dream that motivates and inspires you, and you are in hot pursuit of that dream, you will have a totally different outlook on life.

I love George Bernard Shaw's statement: "Some men see things as they are and say, 'Why?' I dream of things that never were and say, 'Why not?'"

Unfortunately, many people have given up on their dreams. As I travel the country, I meet many people who have stopped dreaming. I ask them to tell me about their dreams, and they can't. They have settled. As young people, they had dreams . . . big dreams. But they let the world beat them down. They probably had friends and family tell them that they weren't being realistic and, ultimately, they gave up on their dreams.

I believe we were created for success, but we become conditioned for failure. We are conditioned to think that we can't achieve things. We are conditioned to think that our dreams will never come true. We are conditioned to think that it's always someone else who grabs life's brass ring. Well, bull! We don't have to settle. We don't have to give up on our dreams! We don't have to fail! We can achieve, we can win, we can change our lives, and we can grab life's brass ring!

RETHINK POSSIBLE

With the opportunities we have before us in network marketing, we need to rethink what is possible in our lives. We need to stop living in the past and realize that the next chapter in our life is unwritten. We can do anything that we set our mind to. Let's take a minute and look back at some examples of people who were willing to rethink possible.

THE FOUNDING FATHERS

On July 4, 1776, the founding fathers of our country, led by Thomas Jefferson, had to rethink possible when they gathered to approve a document that we all know today as the Declaration of Independence.

The founding fathers all grew up where a royal family and an overbearing government was the norm. At the time, Great Britain was the undisputed super power. However, the burning desire of the founding fathers to live free of tyranny and oppression led to the signing of the Declaration of Independence.

Many colonists and most of Great Britain never imagined that this young country would pull it off. However, the founding fathers of the United States of America were not afraid to rethink possible and because of their courage and action, a nation was born.

NASA AND SCIENTIST JOHN CALLAS

When I was a kid, Mars was just a faraway place talked about in comic books, but a scientist named John Callas rethought possible and spearheaded a NASA mission in the summer of 2003 that sent rockets carrying two rovers 34 million miles into space. Their destination was Planet Mars. The two rovers, named Spirit and Opportunity, roamed the Red Planet, sending back data and pictures to scientists here on Earth. I say scientist John Callas and NASA were rethinking possible.

SIR ROGER BANNISTER

In track and field, the experts insisted that breaking the four-minute mile couldn't be done. For decades, runners had been trying without success . . . until a runner named Roger Bannister decided to rethink possible.

On May 6, 1954, Bannister posted a time of 3 minutes, 59.4 seconds and changed the world of track and field competition forever. To show the ripple effect that Roger Bannister created, in the following ten years, 336 other runners broke the four-minute-mile mark.

PHILADELPHIA EAGLE VINCE PAPALE

In professional football, Vince Papale decided to rethink possible; at an age when most players were thinking about retiring, Vince tried out for the Philadelphia Eagles. At the ripe old age of 30, he not only made the team, but he was also voted captain. He became the oldest rookie with no college experience ever to make an NFL team. Because Vince was willing to rethink possible, Disney made the movie *Invincible* about his life, and it has inspired millions of people.

COLONEL SANDERS

When his critics were saying he was too old, Colonel Harland Sanders took $105 from his Social Security check and started the now-famous Kentucky Fried Chicken. Because Colonel Harland Sanders was willing, at age sixty-five, to rethink possible, he left an amazing legacy. He endowed a trust fund that has given millions to help charities and fund scholarships.

I know some of you are thinking that these stories are nice and that some people can change their lives, but not you. To that, I say, "Bull!" You can do anything that you want to do if you are willing to get out of your comfort zone and work hard.

Dream big! Billionaire Donald Trump says, "You have to think anyway, so why not think big?" If there were no stopping your success, and you could have and do anything in your life, what would it be? Successful people form a clear picture of what their dream lives look like. You may want to cut out pictures of your dream house, your dream car, and your dream vacation and place them where you will see them often, such as on the refrigerator or the bathroom mirror. You may even want to create a special dream board to help keep you focused and motivated.

Share a photo of your dream house or car on your Twitter feed and Facebook wall (using #CoachPresley) and let others know what you're striving for!

KEEP YOUR MIND AWARE

Your brain is far more complex and powerful than the world's biggest computer. Make your mind aware of your dreams, and your subconscious will go to work achieving them.

The reason you need to look at your dreams every day is the same reason you need to stay in the company of positive people . . . it helps keep you focused on the right things. If you don't keep yourself constantly focused on your destination, you will be like a ship without a rudder. You will drift off course and never come close to reaching your dreams.

COACH'S SUCCESS TIP:

DON'T SETTLE. DREAM!

We need our dreams. The Bible says that without vision, the people perish. Dreams give us hope. They keep us going when we are brought down by the world. To be a successful networker, you must be a dreamer.

"Where there is no vision, the people perish: but he that keepeth the law, happy is he."

— PROVERBS 29:18 (KJV)

We must rethink possible. What would your perfect life look like? Where would you live? What would you drive? How would you feel? What would you be doing? I know of no one who has built a massively successful network marketing business but doesn't have a clear idea of what it would be like to live his or her dream.

HOMEWORK

1. Grab a pen and paper. At the top of the paper, write "My Life Plan."

2. Start writing down what you want your life to be like in the future. Imagine the possibilities, and be descriptive as you ink your future on paper. If you want to have it, be it, or do it, then it's important to write it down. I find it sad that most people take more time to plan a two-week vacation than they do planning their lives. Don't let that be you.

3. Take time now to write your dreams in these four core areas of your life:

   - Money
   - Relationships
   - Health
   - Personal/Spiritual Growth

4. Share on your Facebook wall and your Twitter feed (be sure to include #CoachPresley) that you are writing down your life plan. Encourage others to do the same, and share a few parts of your plan that might motivate others. Let me know about your life plan as well by posting it to my Facebook wall www.facebook.com/presleyswagerty

I can't emphasize enough how important it is to have a clear vision for what you want and where you're going. This is huge!

CHAPTER 6 – Stepping Stones to Your Dreams

"People with goals succeed because they know where they're going."

— Earl Nightingale

GOAL SETTING

Setting goals is another important factor in laying the foundation for building your business. Dreams are where we want our destination to be, and goals are the road map of how to get there. Goals are steps we take to reach our dreams. Dreams and goals are definitely interrelated. Establishing goals is a must for achieving success and reaching dreams. I could write an entire book on goal setting, but I will try to give you the basic keys in this chapter.

Many people feel they are getting nowhere fast. A big reason they feel this way is that they haven't really decided what they want out of life; they haven't set any goals. We don't fire a gun without a target. We don't set out on a trip without a destination. Yet so many of us live our lives with no clue of where we want to end up!

Goal setting is a powerful tool for thinking about your future and motivating you to turn your dreams into reality. By knowing exactly what you want to achieve in life, you know where to focus your efforts.

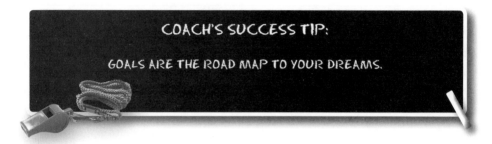

COACH'S SUCCESS TIP:

GOALS ARE THE ROAD MAP TO YOUR DREAMS.

SEVEN STEPS FOR GOAL SETTING

One: Have Goals That Motivate You

The first step in goal setting is to know what you really want and make sure what you want motivates you. Set your sights on something important to you, something that excites you and that will have a huge impact on your life when it happens. If you have little or no interest in the outcome, or if your goals are insignificant in the big picture, then the chances of your putting in the effort to reach them are slim. This is why your goals must be immense and matter deeply to you. They must be big and important enough to you so that no obstacle can prevent or deter you from reaching them! Motivation is a huge key to achieving your goals.

Two: Have Specific, Measurable Goals

Your goals must be clear and well defined. Set precise goals, putting in times, dates, and amounts so you can measure achievement and identify every success en route. Without a way to measure your success, it's impossible to know if you actually reached your goal. Many people dream about being successful, and that's okay, but that's not specific enough—it's too vague.

If you don't have a clear picture of your goal, how will you know when you have reached it? You can say that you are going to work hard today, but there is no real way to measure that, no way to know if you are cheating yourself. However, if you have a goal to make ten calls a day, you have a clear way to measure. Either you make ten calls or you don't.

Here is another example . . . say your goal is to make more money, and the following month you make $100 more. Did you reach your goal? Your goals must give you a distinct target or end to work toward. This instant, clear, and definite feedback gives you all the motivation you need to get out of bed each day and continue pushing toward your goals.

Three: Have Time-Bound Goals

Write goals down with a specific date to achieve the goal. A goal without a deadline is a goal you have not fully committed to and a goal you probably will not achieve. A deadline is simply your best guess of when you will accomplish your goal. It is like aiming a gun at a bull's-eye on a target. You may hit the bull's-eye or you may miss the bull's-eye, but you need the target. If you miss, you make adjustments and shoot again. The same is true with your deadlines; you will hit roughly half of your goal deadlines, and you will miss roughly half of your goal deadlines, but you must have a deadline. If you miss your deadline, make adjustments, pick a new date, and get going again. Realize that even if you have to adjust two or three times, the important thing is that you reached your goal.

If working on a goal is something you can do "whenever," you won't! A deadline will give you that needed sense of urgency.

Four: Have an Action Plan to Reach Your Goals

Your ability to develop a plan for reaching your goals is one of your greatest success skills. No other skill will help you more in fulfilling your potential, and this step is often overlooked in the process of goal setting. You are so focused on the outcome that you forget to establish the steps necessary to reach your goals. Sometimes our big goals seem overwhelming. We rarely see them as a series of small, achievable tasks, but in reality, breaking down a big goal into smaller tasks—and completing them one at a time—is exactly how any big goal gets reached. You have heard the question, "How do you eat an elephant?" The answer is, "One bite at a time." How do you achieve a huge goal? You accomplish it one step, one task, one measure at a time.

After you decide what you really want and set measurable goals with specific time frames, the next step is to determine all of the individual actions you will need to take to accomplish your goal. Here are the steps:

1. Make a list of everything you can think of that you will need to do to reach your goal.
2. Organize your list by priority. What is the most important task or activity? What's the second-most important? And so on.

3. Organize your list by sequence. What must be done before something else can be done?

4. Revisit and revise your plan regularly, especially when new information becomes available or things are not progressing as you had planned. Be prepared to make changes if needed. As you are reviewing your goals, the achievement of the smallest goal is something to be excited about—it shows you are making progress. If you need to change a goal, do not consider it a failure; consider it a victory because you had the insight to realize there was something better.

The purpose of planning is to enable you to turn your major goals into a planned project with specific steps with beginnings, middles, and ends . . . with clear deadlines. Fortunately, this is a skill you can learn and master with a little practice.

Five: Write Everything Down

Writing down your goals creates the roadmap to your success. The physical act of writing down a goal makes it real and tangible. As you write, express your goals as positive statements. "I will accomplish . . ." "I will reach . . ." "I will do . . ." Also, instead of writing "a new home," write, "a 4,000-square-foot traditional house with four bedrooms and three baths with a view of the mountains on ten acres of land." We are giving our subconscious mind a detailed set of instructions to work with.

When you have a clearly defined goal, it activates your subconscious mind on your behalf. Any thought, plan, or goal that you can clearly define in your conscious mind will be brought into reality by your subconscious mind.

We all have within our brain a special organ called the reticular cortex. This part of the brain functions like a switchboard in a company. The calls come in and are routed to the correct person. Just as calls are received and routed, all incoming information to your senses is routed through your reticular cortex to the relevant part of your brain.

Your reticular cortex contains your reticular activating system. When you send a goal message to your reticular cortex, it starts to make you intensely aware of and alert to people, information, and opportunities in your environment. Sending any goal message to your reticular cortex causes your reticular activating system to make you alert to all possible ways to make a goal a reality.

Six: Take Action Daily

If you had a large tree in your backyard and each day you would take five swings with an ax, eventually, no matter how big the tree, it would have to come down. How simple and how true! From this, I came up with what I call the Rule of Five. This simply means that every day you should do five things that will help you reach your goals. And just like the tree coming down, your goals, no matter how big, will be reached! Remember, do five things to reach your goals every day, whether or not you feel like it.

Seven: Never Quit

Once you have determined your goals, resolve in advance that you will persist until you succeed. Make a decision that you will overcome every setback and problem until you achieve your goals. Difficulties come not to obstruct but to instruct. When you resolve in advance to learn from every experience, your ultimate success becomes inevitable. You must stay the course.

TREY DYER'S BIKE RIDE

When I think of goals, I think of Trey Dyer. Trey is a presidential director in our company and, simply put, he's the best of the best when it comes to explaining the importance of goal setting. Trey is so good, in fact, that I refer to him as Yoda—The Master. Trey uses a great story about a charity bike ride when he shares his thoughts on goals. I found that this story brings home the finer points of the importance of goal setting, but it's also an uplifting story. Here's Trey:

Set a Big Goal

Set a goal that will require you to stretch, to grow, to sacrifice, and to become more than you are now. If the goal is too small, you won't be motivated to stretch. Set a goal that will inspire you and ignite your passion.

Riding the MS150

"It's for a great cause," Richard said, "and after all, it's more of a joyride than anything. It'll be fun, and when you cross the finish line, you'll feel like Lance Armstrong!" Richard was a longtime friend and business associate. This was his final pitch as he pushed the laptop with the registration page already loaded, ready for my sign-up to ride the MS150 from Houston to Austin, a two-day bicycle ride to benefit the National Multiple Sclerosis Society.

"Create a world free of MS!" it read at the top of the page. I began typing. This was a great cause, and even if I hadn't bought in, I knew Richard had. He'd been after me for weeks. So what if I hadn't been on a bicycle since before junior high. Remember, he said joyride! Far from it! But I didn't find that out until a week before the ride . . .

Make Your Goal Specific

Even if you doubt your ability to achieve your goal at first, write it down, make it specific, and—yes—it has to have a deadline. Deadlines give you the sense of urgency you need to take action, and action is the catalyst that creates the magic.

"One hundred and fifty miles in two days."

"Houston to Austin."

"Joyride?"

Most of my attention leading up to the ride was spent raising donations from the contacts I had through my network of friends and business associates. "It's a great cause," was my battle cry, and I raised, in just a few days, three times the minimum required to participate. I was proud of myself, but didn't make time to actually train for the ride.

A couple weeks before the ride, I took my borrowed bicycle to a shop near my home to get it checked out. The guy at the store asked what I was using it for and I told him, "I'm riding the MS150 from Houston to Austin. Ever heard of it?" He told me he was well aware of the ride and asked how much training I'd been doing. "Training?" I asked.

"As in how many miles per week have you been riding?" he replied.

"I haven't been doing any. Isn't this just kind of a joyride?"

With a look of concern he said, "Man, you're going to suffer!"

I began to wonder, *What have I gotten myself into?*

Share Your Goals

Share your goals with someone who can help you accomplish them. Find an accountability partner who has similar goals, someone who will push you and help you make mid-course adjustments.

I called my friend Chris, who was also riding, and he suggested we go on a practice ride.

"We'll ride down the highway a little while and you can get some practice." We rode twenty-five miles. After the ride, I got off the bike, crawled into the house, and called Sally, my wife. "Babe, I'm in trouble." Now I was in a panic. "There's no way I can ride 150 miles. What am I going to do?"

Next, I phoned Richard and tried to back out. He wouldn't let me. "Trust me," he said. "You can do it."

As I hung up the phone, the magnitude of what I was about to attempt and the total lack of preparation started to sink in. There was no backing out.

Plan Your Journey

Divide your big goal into intermediate goals that you can measure and celebrate. Reaching these goals will give you a sense of accomplishment and enable you to believe that you can reach the ultimate goal.

Chris and I arrived in Houston the evening before the race and Richard laid out the plans for the next day. "We'll ride one hundred miles tomorrow."

"One hundred miles? I thought we were riding seventy-five miles tomorrow and seventy-five on Sunday."

"We're starting with the rest of the team," he said. "We will do a hundred miles tomorrow and fifty on Sunday. We'll start at the Park-and-Ride and be in Bellville for lunch. From there, we go to La Grange for the night." Richard could tell I was becoming really stressed over hearing this. "You can do it. La Grange will be fun! We'll get a great meal and maybe even a massage," he assured me. "Chris and I will be right there with you the whole way." That didn't make me feel any better!

Define and Commit to Your Daily Activities

Break your intermediate goals into bite-sized activities or daily goals. Then commit to those activities. If you accomplish your daily and weekly objectives and stay persistent, then you will eventually accomplish your ultimate goal. Committing to and accomplishing these small steps are the key to your success.

The morning of the race, the team gathered in the immense parking lot off I-10 in Houston. It was still very dark outside and it even started sprinkling as we listened to the team leaders' final talk before we pedaled off. "I'm really worried about today," I told Richard.

"Oh, it's eleven miles to the first check point. We'll stop there, refill our water bottles, and have a banana. Don't worry about the rest of the day; just make it to the first rest area. Do you think you can go eleven miles?"

"Sure, I can go that far." As we started on our journey, the butterflies in my stomach disappeared. The first leg didn't seem too tiring. As we pulled into the first rest stop, Richard asked, "How ya feelin'?"

"Good! That wasn't so bad."

As we refilled our water bottles, he said, "Next rest stop, fourteen miles."

As we pulled out onto the highway, I noticed all the riders funneling into the rest stop. Some 13,000 cyclists would stop there that day. What a huge event!

The second leg wasn't much more difficult than the first. I was getting more comfortable riding in the group and felt like we were really accomplishing something. We were a river of cyclists riding for a great cause. At the second rest stop, there were vendors and even a band playing classic rock songs! This ride was starting to get fun.

"Next rest stop, eleven miles." Remember, bite-sized activities.

Track Your Results and Celebrate Your Victories

Reviewing your results gives you the ability to make mid-course corrections and keeps you on the right track. Rewarding yourself when reaching intermediate goals keeps you motivated and energized.

As the day wore on, we repeated the same routine over and over—always pedaling for the next rest stop. At lunch in Bellville, we talked about how many legs we'd completed and how many we had to go. I was surprised at how good I felt, and I started to believe that I could actually finish the hundred miles for Day 1. When we rolled into La Grange that afternoon, I breathed a sigh of relief.

"One day down, one to go."

I was exhausted but also excited. We treated ourselves to barbecue, ice cream, a massage, and a shower. "I can't even imagine the pain of trying to get back on that bike tomorrow morning," I whined.

"Don't worry about tomorrow," Richard soothed. "Just soak in the moment!"

Keep Your Eye on the Prize

Keep your dream in the forefront of your mind. Visualize often what it will be like when you accomplish it. This pulls you through the tough times. With any big goal, you'll encounter obstacles, sometimes even seemingly insurmountable hurdles. By keeping your eye on the prize, you can overcome almost anything.

The next morning, getting back on the bike wasn't nearly as tough as I thought it would be. "Today you're going to feel like Lance Armstrong," Richard said as he clipped in and pushed off. With the addition of a few more hills, the ride was a repeat of the day before. "How many miles until the next rest stop?" was the phrase of the day. We took turns drafting off each other and even raced down a hill or two. Throughout the ride, there were small signs every few miles reminding us of why we were riding — "Pedaling for a Cure." "The cure is just another mile ahead" was another slogan. At every intersection, there were police stopping traffic, always giving us encouragement. Through every town, people were lined up to clap and cheer. And when we got to Austin, people were lining the streets to the finish line cheering as we rode by . . . feeling just like Lance Armstrong! After the ride, we celebrated with friends who had driven to Austin to see us finish. It was an awesome feeling, one I will never forget.

> The MS150 was one of the most rewarding and grueling experiences I've had. I'll never forget the feeling of accomplishment after pedaling 150 miles. I wouldn't recommend attempting it without training, but it illustrates that by taking a goal and breaking it down into manageable activities, and then committing to those activities, anything can be accomplished.
>
> —Trey Dyer

DAILY TO-DO LIST

An important side note on goal setting is a daily to-do list or daily goals list. Decide each day what you want to accomplish, and work with a purpose because either you run the day or the day runs you. Having a daily to-do list keeps you organized and is vital to your success. Before you go to bed each night, make a list of everything that you want to accomplish the next day. Prioritize the list in order of importance so that when you open your eyes in the morning, you hit the ground running. This list helps you achieve your short-term goals, which in turn, helps you reach your long-term goals and your dreams. I have found that I get so much more accomplished each day when I'm working from my daily to-do list than when I just let the wind blow me in different directions.

I hope that you now understand the importance of having dreams and setting goals. If you don't already set goals, do so. Start now. As you make goal-setting part of your life, you'll achieve networking success.

COACH'S SUCCESS TIP:

EITHER YOU RUN THE DAY OR THE DAY RUNS YOU.

HOMEWORK

1. Grab a sheet of paper and a pen and complete this powerful exercise. On the top of the page, write "My Goals."

2. Look back at your homework from the last chapter—Dreams. Copy each dream down, and under each dream, make a list of everything that you need to do to reach that dream. Your goals.

3. When you're finished with the list for each dream, ask yourself this powerful question: "Which one of these goals, if it were to be accomplished *now*, would have the greatest impact on my life?"

Whichever goal that is, it should stick out to you. It will have the greatest impact and could help you achieve some of the others on the list. Make this one goal your absolute obsession! Some refer to this as your definite chief aim. But whatever you want to call it, make it your duty that you will achieve this goal. Laser your focus. Get serious about this goal, and start taking action right away. Write your number-one goal in your Twitter feed (include #CoachPresley), Facebook wall and website. You'll be surprised how powerful you are when you concentrate your mind and actions on a single purpose! I'd be grateful as well if you would share your number-one goal on my Facebook wall www.facebook.com/presleyswagerty.

CHAPTER 7 – Hard Work and Perseverance Pay Off

*"It is not the critic who counts, not the man who points out
how the strong man stumbled, or where the doer of deeds
could have done them better. The credit belongs to the man
who is actually in the arena; whose face is marred by dust and
sweat and blood; who strives valiantly; who errs and comes
short again and again; who knows the great enthusiasms, the
great devotions, and spends himself in a worthy cause; who, at
best, knows in the end the triumph of high achievement; and
who, at worst, if he fails, at least fails while daring greatly, so
that his place shall never be with those cold and timid souls
who knew neither victory nor defeat."*

—Theodore Roosevelt

STORY OF THE LUNCHBOX

There once were two hard-hat construction workers who paused to take their lunch break. Both had brought lunchboxes from home. The first worker sat down and flipped open his lunchbox. His face immediately lit up with a big smile, "Yum!" he says. "Bacon, lettuce, and tomato sandwich! My favorite!" He grabbed his sandwich and began to munch down his meal. The second hard-hat worker sat down next to his buddy and popped open his lunch box. "No!" he explodes. "Peanut butter sandwich? Peanut butter sandwich! I'm sick and tired of peanut butter sandwiches!" With a mouthful of food, the happy worker said, "Listen, why not just tell your wife that you don't like peanut butter sandwiches?" Immediately, the angry worker fired back, "Hey, you leave my wife out of this! I pack my own lunch!"

From this simple story, we're reminded that you and I are each responsible for our own lives and that in life, you and I pack our own lunches! We're reminded that our current situation (what's inside our lunchbox) is a result of the thoughts and actions we've taken up to this point in time. But isn't it comforting to know that we can change our situation by having new thoughts, taking new actions, and by adopting a personal philosophy of hard work and perseverance? That's what this chapter is all about.

To be successful requires action. Action usually means a lot of hard work for an extended period . . . but it is worth it. Hard work is the basic building block of success. Without hard work, everything else is pointless. You start with dreams, and then set goals. However, before any success can be realized, you must add lots of hard work.

In America, most of us have been conditioned to think that everything is supposed to be fun. However, hard work is not always fun. That's why it's called work. You've probably heard the saying: "The harder I work, the luckier I get." That's so true. We create our success with effort. It's not about special ability; it's about action.

Discipline is doing what you are supposed to do when you are supposed to do it . . . whether you feel like it or not. Challenge yourself to complete tasks that you really don't want to do—first. Get them behind you. Good habits create discipline in our lives, and it's impossible to achieve success without having discipline.

We are looking for daily successes. Our long-term success is a result of our small, daily accomplishments. You may have big dreams and goals, but they won't do you any good until you execute.

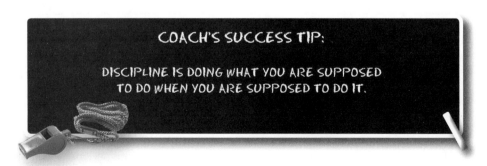

COACH'S SUCCESS TIP:

DISCIPLINE IS DOING WHAT YOU ARE SUPPOSED TO DO WHEN YOU ARE SUPPOSED TO DO IT.

WORK WITH THE END IN MIND

Many of us have heard the story of the man walking down the sidewalk who happened upon three construction workers laying bricks. "What are you doing?" the pedestrian asked the first worker. "Laying bricks, of course," was his reply. "What are you doing?" he asked the second worker. "Building a strong wall," responded the second person. Finally, he asked the third, "And what are you doing?" "Me? I'm building a grand cathedral!"

In this short narrative lies the secret to why work can be a pleasure. Great achievers seem to love what they do. Consider the three bricklayers. Each of them was working, but you can imagine that the third man was much more excited, driven, and happy in his work. Why? Because he wasn't just laying bricks, he was building a grand cathedral! In others words, he was focused on the big picture: the END RESULT.

In our network marketing business, I believe we're not really working. Rather, I believe we're changing our life and our family's lives! I believe we're not just making phone calls. Rather, we're offering hope and opportunity to our friends and family! These beliefs make it a pleasure to work.

What makes the day-to-day grind more enjoyable is keeping the end in mind. If the vision is clear, the price is easy. So if we can keep a clear picture of the finish line, where we're going, and why we're doing the business, then the price we pay is easy in comparison. Tie this idea into writing down your goals. I bet you can now see why writing down your goals is so important and why having a vision board or pictures of the things you want on the refrigerator is so crucial. Anything we can do to keep the end result in mind will cause the work we do to be easier and more enjoyable. With our compelling vision in mind, we'll pay whatever price. It's as if we are being helped or pulled toward our goals like a magnet!

Don't forget to use your social media as a tool for an online vision board. Use #CoachPresley on Twitter and Facebook.

LOWERING THE TARGET VS. INCREASING THE ACTIVITY

Since we're talking about goals in relation to work, now is a good time to warn you what NOT to do.

Most people set goals and begin to work toward those goals. Inevitably, however, they soon come across hardship, setbacks, and difficulties, all of which accompany any worthwhile ambition. And what do most people do at this point of difficulty? Well, if they don't quit, most decide to LOWER their target.

Here's an example. Let's say that John joins a network marketing company and decides that he wants to earn $2,000 a month part-time. After a few weeks of getting some rejection from his friends and family, John decides that instead of $2,000 a month he'd be happy with just $500 a month from his new part-time networking business. What did John do? John lowered his target. He settled. He backed down from his dream. He went from a compelling initial dream of $2,000 a month to settling for scraps: $500 a month.

There's a second option that few consider, and that is to increase your activity. Rather than lowering the target, make the decision to increase the amount of activity to reach the goal you desire. Consider whether, when you initially set your goal, you simply underestimated the amount of effort it was going to take to get there. You're not alone. Most people underestimate everything in life, so chances are you've simply underestimated what it takes to win. Rather than lowering your target (a nice way of saying that you settled for less than your potential), it's time you look at this second option: increase your activity.

Here's an example. Imagine that Joe wants to sponsor two new associates per month. When setting that goal, he estimated that one out of three would say yes to his business. But after presenting for a few months, Joe realizes he's only getting one of six to sign up. So rather than lowering his target, he simply needs to increase activity and accept that only one in six will sign. So Joe now decides he'll find a way to show twelve people a month so he can achieve his goal.

In summary, don't settle by lowering your target. That's what everyone else does. Instead, do what winners do—find ways to increase your activity to achieve your dreams.

TRACK YOUR ACTIONS, NOT YOUR INTENTIONS

In his book, *The Game of Work*, Charles Coonradt says, "Feedback is the breakfast of champions." He also states, "All winners are trackers."

Randy Hedge tells his leaders, "Track activity, not intentions." This is such an important concept. If you're like me, you wake up with wonderful intentions for the day: "I'm going to make ten calls, I'm going to talk to my neighbor, I'm going to give a brochure to my coworker," and any other intentions you have. But, as the day progresses, oftentimes our actions don't match those intentions. This ultimately is the reason for the lack of progress for many well-intentioned teammates in our profession. They mean well, but if you were to track their actions, not their intentions, the reason for their failure would be apparent. We overcome all this by tracking activity. Here are a few good activities to track:

1. How many appointments did I set this week?
2. How many times did I show a business plan this week?
3. How many new potential customers did I talk to this week?

The only things that pay in networking are income-producing activities. As you consider what to track in your networking business, my recommendation is to track what makes you money.

There's nothing as motivating as progress. Tracking gives you feedback . . . and consistent feedback, over time, can show you your progress. And progress is exciting! Try this for a few weeks, and you'll find self-motivation through this simple idea of tracking your income-producing activities. Remember: good intentions don't pay the mortgage; stay focused on activity (not intentions), and you'll soon find yourself on the road to financial freedom!

A STORY ABOUT A HARD-CHARGING LEADER, ROGER FESTA

A hard-charging leader on my team, Roger Festa, was a champion of the importance of income-producing activity and taking action. Roger was a war hero, and he brought that tenacity to his networking business. He was always taking action and going places.

We recently lost Roger very unexpectedly. While we miss our friend and his take-charge, hard-driving style, Roger's memory lives on with a legacy that includes many lives touched by his message. His dear wife, Ann, shares her thoughts on Roger's special way of focusing on income-producing activities, including a daily to-do list and why we need to make every day count.

Roger always wanted to live every day to the fullest with no regrets. He wanted to go hard to the finish line and accomplish something every day. He considered himself a proactive person—willing to take the first step rather than to wait for someone else to determine his destiny.

As a part of his daily routine, Roger would get up early and review his list of things to accomplish that day. He was focused on getting as many things accomplished as he could each day and needed his list so he did not get off track and forget the priorities he had set for himself.

Roger always had his list of income-producing activities as his highest priority. Having been an entrepreneur most of his life, he knew that no one was going to send him a check unless he put out the effort to make it happen. Roger didn't believe in the entitlement world we live in today. He was willing to work under a success model where he was rewarded for what he did. Roger wanted to change the "think tank" philosophy into the "do tank." Roger was a take-charge person and wanted to inspire all the people around him to take matters into their own hands if they wanted to succeed.

—Ann Festa

COACH'S SUCCESS TIP:

PROCRASTINATION IS THE BIGGEST STEALER OF DREAMS.

One thing I discovered through athletics is that we can do more than we think. Anyone who has won a championship or achieved anything significant in life has pushed harder and done more that he or she thought possible.

TEAM USA

Consider the sport of hockey and Team USA's improbable gold medal run at the 1980 Winter Olympics. I remember exactly where I was when history was made on February 22, 1980, when the young, scrappy Americans took down the powerhouse hockey team from the USSR, the Red Machine.

After participating in not one, but two, Olympics as a player, Herb Brooks spent the 1970s as head coach at the University of Minnesota. There, Brooks led the Gophers to NCAA titles on three separate occasions. He became known for his relentless attention to preparation. His experience, coupled with his keen interest in international hockey, created the perfect scenario for Herb to lead a group of young men to do something very special in the world of hockey.

The USSR, after a tough run in the mid-1970s, had battled back to return to the top spot in the world of hockey. A year before the 1980 Lake Placid Games, the Soviets had whipped the NHL All Stars 6–0 in the final game of a series. The idea that a bunch of wannabes had even a remote chance to knock off these disciplined athletes from the Soviet Union seemed wishful thinking at best. Even so, Brooks was undeterred. Coach Brooks spent over a year building the team. He painstakingly sifted and sorted through several hundred prospects from which the team was finally selected.

Knowing the Europeans possessed superior skills, Brooks focused on what he knew best: preparation and hard work. He drilled the team for hours, honing their speed and conditioning. In other words, he decided to out-work and be more mentally tough than his competition. The team was disciplined. He focused on teaching his team to capitalize on opportunities. He also challenged them physically and verbally. He constantly reminded them that they were tough enough and good enough to accomplish what most said was impossible. He reminded them over and over that they must believe in themselves and each other. He instilled in them a winning attitude and the belief that they could accomplish winning Olympic gold.

While the Soviets embarked on a final, desperate charge, commentator Al Michaels proclaimed, "Eleven seconds. You got ten seconds. The countdown is going on right now. Five seconds left in the game! Do you believe in miracles? Yes!" As time expired, the stands erupted! That dramatic win is what most people call the "Miracle on Ice."

While most pundits cite scoring heroics, the American victory would not have been possible without sheer determination, belief, and total commitment. It is amazing what we can accomplish when we make a commitment. I believe that once we make a decision and reinforce that decision by taking action consistently and deliberately for a period of time, anything is possible. I believe that great and mighty forces will come to our aid when we make a true commitment. And I think the U.S. upset of the Soviets in 1980 is a perfect example of that.

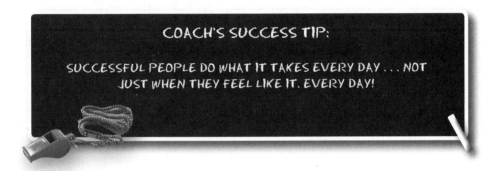

COACH'S SUCCESS TIP:

SUCCESSFUL PEOPLE DO WHAT IT TAKES EVERY DAY . . . NOT JUST WHEN THEY FEEL LIKE IT. EVERY DAY!

"Great works are performed not by strength but by perseverance."

— **SAMUEL JOHNSON**

PERSEVERANCE

Perseverance is refusing to give up—refusing to quit. Perseverance makes you great and enables you to perform at your highest level and reach your dreams. Perseverance allows you to raise the bar and then establish the steps necessary to reach new heights.

Those who lack perseverance start out with the best intentions, but lose focus and eventually give up on their dreams. Perseverance is the critical factor in your networking success. All other traits can be acquired or learned with time. However, unless you persevere through every obstacle, you will never have a chance to achieve financial freedom.

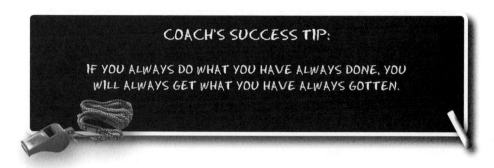

COACH'S SUCCESS TIP:

IF YOU ALWAYS DO WHAT YOU HAVE ALWAYS DONE, YOU WILL ALWAYS GET WHAT YOU HAVE ALWAYS GOTTEN.

WHY NOT ME?

When things aren't going your way, it is easy to ask, "Why me?" But the better question is, "Why not me?" Networking is our chance to change our lives. I don't care how hard it gets, never give up! Never give in! Never quit! Remember . . . pain is temporary; quitting is forever.

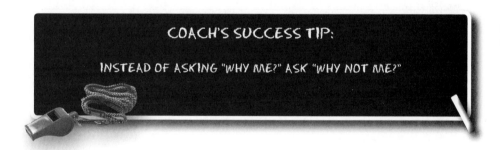

COACH'S SUCCESS TIP:

INSTEAD OF ASKING "WHY ME?" ASK "WHY NOT ME?"

It's time that we all renew our spirit and take advantage of this opportunity. We live in America. We can all be, do, and have so much more, but to achieve all that's possible, we must attempt the impossible; to be all that we can be, we must dream of being more.

Once a month, post your positive answer to "Why not me?" to your Facebook and Twitter. Use #CoachPresley.

HOMEWORK

I finished this chapter talking about having a big dream, a vision for your future. If your vision is clear and compelling, then you'll gladly pay the price. This exercise will help you with this process. Moreover, this exercise can change your life!

Grab a sheet of paper. In large bold letters, write "What I Want." And next to this, write down a specific goal you have. This could be anything: a specific income, a rank advancement, a dream home, a car you desire, a better relationship, anything. Whatever it is, make sure it's clear. And write it in bold letters.

Example: What I Want: A Promotion to Executive Director in my Company.

Next, on the same piece of paper, underneath what you just wrote, write **"The Price I Will Gladly Pay."** Below this header, write out the bullet points of what it's going to take, the price you're willing to pay to get what you want.

Example: The Price I Will Gladly Pay:

1. **Sacrifice every lunch break I have to meet with one person.**

2. **Turn off the radio during my commute home so I can call two people.**

3. **Wake up fifteen minutes earlier and read ten pages out of a good book.**

4. **Drop the bowling league for twelve months and spend those Thursday nights building my future.**

Finally, decide now that you'll pay that price. You've written out clearly what you want. You know the price it's going to take. So commit. Decide now that you will gladly pay the price because you know what it is you want. Tweet to your followers—or write an entry on your Facebook wall or website—the thing you are giving up and the reason. For example, "You won't see me at morning coffee anymore; I am taking that time for the next two weeks to update my contact list!"

You can repeat these three steps for a second or even a third goal you might have. But doing this just for your PRIMARY goal is oftentimes enough to turn your life around drastically. This exercise can change your life, if you'll follow through and pay the price. The good news is that if your goal is clear and compelling, you will gladly pay the price because you know it will be worth it!

CHAPTER 8 – Start Now!

"If we don't start, it's certain we can't arrive."

—ZIG ZIGLAR

"The scariest moment is always just before you start."

—STEPHEN KING

You have embarked on a journey that has changed the personal and financial lives of millions of people just like you. In this chapter, you will learn how people from all walks of life are succeeding in the network marketing profession. The ideas in this book, combined with your personal diligence and determination, are all you need to succeed. I believe you can accomplish all your personal and financial goals if you put your mind and heart into it.

Before we get started, I want you to make four commitments:

1. **Get in the game.** If you don't make time to get plugged in, you can't expect anything to change. You must get involved in business presentations and trainings. If you don't have local meetings, plug into your company webinars and conference calls. Also, plan to attend regional and national events. In networking, you have to "show up to go up." Plugging in is not optional if you want massive success.

2. **Follow your company's system.** My objective is not to tell you which system to use in your business. There are many different, but equally effective, systems for growing a large team and creating wealth. The more important question is whether you have a system at all. Achieving success in your business is very simple: follow the system provided by your company. Follow the system, and you will have the experience of your entire company's leadership as your guide. In other words, don't try to reinvent the wheel. Someone has already blazed the trail for you. You are paid to imitate and not to create.

3. **Be prepared for a marathon.** Be prepared to make a long-term commitment to your business if you want to see big results. Be prepared for a marathon and not a sprint. Make a commitment to see the job through to the end. The biggest hurdle between you and success will be a lack of commitment. While you will have good days and bad days, good weeks and bad weeks, there will be many successes along the way if you stay committed and keep your eye on the prize.

4. **Take massive and immediate action.** The most successful people in the world are those who take what they learn and immediately put it to action. The world is full of people who are planning to get started but never do. "Now" is the magic word of success. Tomorrow, next week, next month, next year, and someday are most often synonyms for never. Lots of good dreams never come true because we say, "I'll start someday," when we should say, "I'll start now!" Get with your sponsor or an upline leader, and start gathering customers and showing the business presentation to your contacts now. It is much easier to build a team quickly than it is to build slowly. Get in gear and go!

COMMITMENT

We all do pretty much the same things every day. We sleep, eat, think, play, feel, talk, listen, etc. We each have twenty-four hours a day, 8,760 hours a year. Winners and losers both do the same basic things in their lives. Yet the things winners do take them to the top, while the things losers do take them to the bottom. So, what's the difference? Winners understand commitment. Once you understand commitment, then you will take the necessary steps to reach your dreams. If you don't change your thinking and make a commitment, no number of how-tos will help you. The reason how-to books and courses don't work for most people isn't that the actions are wrong. It's that people don't keep doing them . . . they don't stay the course. Focusing on the actions is not enough; it's the commitment behind the actions that keeps those actions in place long enough for an individual to be successful.

If you really want to change your life through network marketing, you must make a commitment. You must keep telling yourself that all the meetings, all the webinars, all the appointments that you set, and all the business presentations that you do are going to be worth it. What price can you put on financial freedom?

 Share your winning commitments to your Facebook and Twitter using #CoachPresley.

MY TURNING POINT

There was a time early on when I was in the business, but not really "in" the business. I was playing with it. I knew it was a good idea. I certainly knew I needed it. But, for whatever reason, I hadn't made a total commitment. I decided to go to the annual company convention. However, after making a couple of calls to some other associates, I soon realized that I had waited too long and the convention had sold out. I didn't think I was going to be able to attend.

However, at the last minute, someone cancelled. As fate would have it, I got a ticket to my first major networking event. It turned out to be a huge turning point in my life.

I still remember where I was sitting as I watched the top money earners walk across the stage. I remember sitting there, along with thousands of other associates, and thinking, "I'm supposed to be on that stage!"

I left that event with a resolve like none I had ever experienced. I made a decision that I would never again be sitting in the audience at a major event. I made a true commitment to myself that I would be on the stage, being recognized for making money and changing lives!

I don't know where you will be when your turning point comes, but I do know that when you make a commitment, everything will change for you. You must understand that if you really want to make life-changing income, you MUST make a commitment.

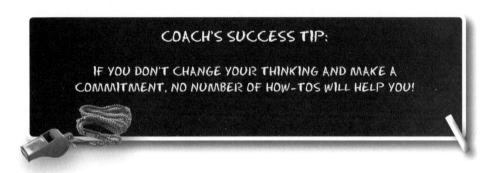

COACH'S SUCCESS TIP:

IF YOU DON'T CHANGE YOUR THINKING AND MAKE A
COMMITMENT, NO NUMBER OF HOW-TOS WILL HELP YOU!

PREGAME

Okay, you have now made a commitment, and so it's time to get started. Here are your five pregame steps to success:

1. **Get with your sponsor and get enrolled.** One of the attributes of successful people is that they can make a decision. Call your sponsor and get going. Your sponsor should walk you through this. Notice I didn't say that your sponsor would do it for you. You need to know the process so you can walk your new associates through the sign-up process.
2. **Set up your website.** Websites are typically replicated and look the same or similar for all associates. It is your presence on the World Wide Web. You now have your portal to sign up associates and customers.
3. **Become your own first customer.** If you are going to sell Fords, you need to drive a Ford. Start ordering products or get on the service.
4. **Get one outside customer.** Your first outside customer should be the one person in your life most interested in helping you succeed. A lot of times, this is Mom, Dad, or a best friend. Getting a customer under your belt gives you confidence.

5. Know your "Why." To be successful in your networking business, you must have something that you are passionate about, something that drives you to keep going when times get tough. I call this your "why." Your why is your reason for starting your network marketing business. I can teach you how to do the business, but you must know why you are doing the business. Your why is the fuel that powers your networking engine. If you are not motivated by a strong why, you will not stay the course and see the job through. Your why should be so compelling to you personally that you fear failure more than you fear any obstacle or person. It may be staying home with your kids, supplementing your retirement, helping elderly parents, becoming financially free, or millions of other whys. Whatever it is, it must be big enough to keep you going, even when things aren't as smooth as you would like. If your why is big enough, you will figure out how. So, what is your why? Take a couple of minutes to write it down.

LEARN BY DOING

How do you learn by doing? Go out and gain experience in the field. This is a learn-as-you-go or earn-while-you-learn business. Follow the leadership of your upline, but get in the game. An experienced leader will show you the potholes to avoid as well as the vast potential of your business.

PROCLAIM YOURSELF

Call your sponsor and upline leaders and introduce yourself. Let them know your story. Tell them your why and let them know you have made a commitment to follow the system, be coachable, and take action. A call like this from a new associate is music to a sponsor's or upline leader's ears. Set up a time to sit down with your sponsor or an upline leader and get some coaching. Ask them to help you share the information with your first few prospects, so you can learn by watching them in action. Now you are ready to embark on developing the skills we will discuss in the pages ahead.

COACH'S SUCCESS TIP:

WORKING TOGETHER WITH AN EXPERIENCED LEADER WILL DRASTICALLY INCREASE YOUR RATE OF SUCCESS.

HOMEWORK

1. Don't just read this book. Be the type of person who applies it. Pause and go back a few pages and complete the five Pregame Steps to Success outlined in this chapter.

2. Write the word "Commitment" on the top of a blank sheet of paper. Look the word up in the dictionary and write down the definition.

3. Next, imagine for a moment someone who was totally committed to your chosen business. Imagine what that person looks like. How would that person act? What would that person do? What would he or she read? How would he or she talk or interact with others? What energy level would that person have? How would that person dress at the meetings? How would that person carry himself or herself? What would a day in the life of a fully committed person look like?

4. Decide that YOU will be that fully committed person. Why not fully commit? Why not become a top money earner? Why not be the one everyone talks about? Why not be the person who inspires others? Why not?

5. Post the following to your Twitter and Facebook wall: "Today, I became a fully committed person." (Remember to include #CoachPresley) When others ask you what you mean, share your commitment and energy . . . and invite them to be a part of your new, fully committed business.

CHAPTER 9 – Finding the Right People

"If you do what you've always done, you'll get what you've always gotten."

— ANTHONY ROBBINS

Billionaire Stewart Rahr was recently interviewed for Forbes Magazine. In the interview, he revealed that finding the right people has been the key to building a company that brings in $5 billion a year. Here is the gist of what he said: "The key to my success has been to involve the best people I possibly can. Then, I leave it up to those people to go out and find their best people." Although he is referencing his pharmaceutical company, our network marketing business should be built the same exact way. We must recruit the best people we possibly can. After that, we teach them to recruit the best people they possibly can.

WHOM SHOULD I RECRUIT?

You will not always know who is ready or right for your business. Some of the people you think would be perfect for the business may not feel the same way. Other prospects, with no prior record of success, may now be willing to do what it takes to win. Some may not know what they want. They might begin as a customer or get off to a slow start as an associate. Some who start slowly will eventually become leaders. We just don't know.

A good rule of thumb is not to discount anyone. However, we only have so many hours in a day. With that in mind, start with prospects who have demonstrated they have what it takes to be a success. In other words, they have been successful in another business or activity. Keep in mind that success doesn't just come in business. Civic leadership, serving at church, or playing a community role may also be great indicators of success and influence.

THE LIST

Let's start by making a list. The prospect list is the biggest asset in your network marketing business. Building it is one of your most important tasks. I believe that you should make only one list—not a business opportunity list and a customer list. Make one list with everybody whom you have ever known. Begin by writing down the names and phone numbers of your first one hundred contacts. When compiling your list, keep two things in mind: prospect up and never prejudge.

PROSPECT UP

Prospect up means prospecting people more successful and more influential than you are. Focus on movers and shakers who get things done, and you will build an empire. Like E.F. Hutton, when they talk, people listen. Think about it like this: if you were going to invest $100,000 in a business venture, whom would you want for your managing partner? That's the person you want in your networking business as well. They say a leopard can't change its spots, so don't expect broke Uncle Harry to be your top associate. After all, broke Uncle Harry is usually broke for a reason!

On the other hand, if you target self-motivated people with a record of success, then you can expect them to duplicate that success in your networking business. Successful people have large spheres of influence and can be great networkers. Their work ethic and experience will prove very valuable to your team.

I always tell associates, "If you think you are an eight on the socioeconomic scale, then prospect nines and tens. Because if you are an eight and you go for sixes, then that teaches your sixes to go for fours and your fours to go for twos. Pretty soon, you have a whole team of zeroes." Always prospect up!

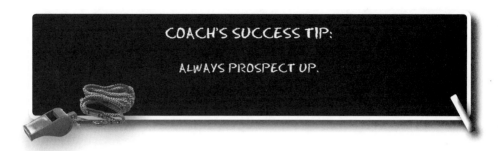

COACH'S SUCCESS TIP:

ALWAYS PROSPECT UP.

NEVER PREJUDGE

Experience has shown that you never know who will or won't be interested. Therefore, give everyone a chance to make his or her own decision. Don't edit your list, or you will edit your success. You can't tell by looking if someone is ready to change his or her life. As the old saying goes, "The ones who you think won't, will, and the ones who you think will, won't." Talk to everybody. I learned that the hard way.

COACH'S SUCCESS TIP:

NEVER PREJUDGE.

THE TOM WESTBROOK STORY

My Sunday school teacher was a man named Tom Westbrook. Tom is a friend of mine for whom I have the utmost respect. Tom drove a Mercedes. When we went golfing, Tom insisted on paying for the round. He was a successful man.

When I got involved in networking, I thought, "Tom's already successful; he wouldn't want to mess with this." So, Tom was on my list, but I didn't call him. He stayed on what I call my chicken list. I didn't call, didn't call, didn't call.

As I recollect, I had been involved with my company for about three months at the time of this story. I was working the business diligently. As I look back, it becomes clear: I was talking to people who I thought needed a break more than I was talking to people who were already successful. Why? Because I was scared to pick up the phone and call my successful friends.

I walked into a meeting one evening and glanced to my left. To my surprise, Tom was sitting there with another guy. If you want to get a sinking feeling in the pit of your stomach, let somebody on your list whom you've been scared to call show up at a meeting with somebody else.

Now, here's the sad part for me. Tom's team exploded! Hundreds of people joined, and he could have easily been in my group if I would have called him. That evening, when he saw me, Tom actually said, "So, you're doing this?"

I said, "Yeah."

He said, "My gosh, why haven't you talked to me?"

I felt about half an inch tall and, to this day, it's still a story that gives me a sick feeling every time I think about it.

That story shows us that we should talk to everybody. Let the prospect make the decision as to whether the business is right for him or her. I have found that successful people are successful for a reason. They see opportunity and they seize opportunity. Put successful people at the top of your list and call them first.

MAKE THE LIST LARGE

You want a large list of potential business partners. If you increase the number of people on your list, it decreases the impact of rejection. If you have five people on your list and three say no, it's devastating. If you have one hundred on your list and three say no, it's no big deal. Start by writing down everyone you can think of off the top of your head.

You should constantly be adding new contacts to your list. Work toward increasing your list daily. Every day, most people meet a new person or two.

Add them to your list. You never know when a new acquaintance is going to be your next superstar.

FRANK

Something that can help build your contact list is to use the acronym FRANK: friends, relatives, associates, neighbors, and kids. Start by writing down your friends and relatives, even the ones you haven't talked to in a while. Next, list your work associates, both past and present. Include your neighbors, and don't forget your kids' friends and their families. FRANK will help jog your memory and grow your list. Don't forget the people with whom you do business. If you do business with someone, he or she should do business with you. Use the memory joggers below to get your list to 100+ names.

COACH'S SUCCESS TIP:

USE A MEMORY JOGGER WHEN LIST BUILDING.

NAME ASSOCIATION

Name association is another great way to add to your prospect list. The following tool may assist you with name associations.

NAME ASSOCIATION TOOL				
Aaron	Clyde	Glen	Kris	Peggy
Al	Cindy	Gwen	Kyle	Penny
Alisa	Connie	Harvey	Kelly	Peter
Amy	Cornelius	Hal	Kim	Phil
Angela	Claudia	Harry	Larry	Rebecca
Andy	Cheryl	Hank	Lauren	Richard
Ann	Dave	Helen	Lance	Roger
Alex	Darlene	Heather	Len	Ray
Alice	Dale	Irene	Linda	Rita
Allison	Don	Ilene	Lorna	Ruth

NAME ASSOCIATION TOOL

Arnold	Donna	Ivan	Luke	Robert
Arthur	Dorothy	Jamie	Lynn	Ron
Barbara	Dot	Jack	Lillian	Rhonda
Ben	Davis	Jake	Lucille	Rick
Beth	Douglas	Jason	Lydia	Samantha
Betty	Daniel	James	Michael	Sam, Samuel
Beverly	Debbie	Jan	Marvin	Stan
Bill	Drew	Jay	Martin	Steve
Brad	Earl	Janice	Marty	Sara
Brian	Ed	Jessica	Mark	Sharon
Bruce	Emma	Jeannette	Matthew	Tom
Burt	Eric	Jennifer	Melissa	Ted
Bonnie	Erica	Jerry	Michelle	Terry
Bob	Eileen	Jean	Mick	Troy
Barry	Ellen	Joan	Mitch	Toby
Betsy	Esther	Joanne	Nancy	Todd
Brandon	Ethel	Joseph	Nathan	Tony
Cecil	Elizabeth	Jodie	Neil	Teresa
Cathy	Elsie	Joel	Ned	Trudy
Cal	Frank	John	Nick	Valerie
Craig	Frances	Josh	Nicholas	Vince
Carl	Floyd	Jonathan	Nina	Vivian
Chris	Gabriel	June	Norma	Wally
Christopher	Gayle	Karen	Norm	Walter
Clark	Gary	Kristin	Pam	Wendy
Curtis	Grace	Kay	Paula	Wayne
Carol	George	Karl	Patricia	Wanda
Charles	Gene	Ken	Patrick	William
Chuck	Greg	Keith	Paul	

OCCUPATION ASSOCIATION

Here is another technique for list building: occupation association.

OCCUPATION ASSOCIATION TOOL		
Physician	Mortician	Brewery Salesperson
Nurse	Missionary	Engineer
Golf Pro	Realtor	Contractor
Student	Karate Instructor	Chiropractor
Model	Editor	Podiatrist
Security Guard	Foreman	Auctioneer
Sheriff	Roofer	Optometrist
Fire Chief	Furniture Salesperson	Pediatrician
Secretary	Air Traffic Controller	Electrician
Welder	Lifeguard	Plumber
Crane Operator	Swim Instructor	Architect
Store Owner	Interior Decorator	Attorney
Police Officer	Computer Salesperson	Dentist
Music Teacher	Grocery Store Owner	Shoe Repairperson
Art Instructor	Insurance Adjustor	Therapist
Forester	Warehouse Manager	Hotel Manager
Seamstress	Mover	State Patrol
Carpenter	Rental Car Rep	Judge
Pilot	Flight Attendant	Photographer
Bus Driver	Radio Announcer	Car Dealer
Bank Teller	Tool and Die Maker	Pizza Delivery Person
Brick Mason	Cookware Sales	Ski Instructor
Detective	Book Salesperson	Hardware Salesperson
Dance Instructor	Car Wash Owner	Phlebotomist
Restaurant Owner	Engineer	Stereo Salesperson
Social Worker	Telephone Repairperson	Caterer
Veterinarian	Video Store Owner	Waitress
Printer	Office Manager	Notary Public
Boat Salesperson	Bakery Owner	Farmer
Coin Dealer	Actor/Actress	Dietician
Landscaper	Mechanic	Anesthetist
Statistician	Surgeon	Librarian

RECRUITING

Once you have a names list underway, you must begin the ongoing exercise of talking to people about your business. Make it as automatic in your day as breathing. If you develop this skill to the point you do it effortlessly as you go about life, the results can change your finances dramatically.

Keep in mind that we are only looking for people who are looking. We are looking for people who want to do something special with their lives.

Network marketing is about timing. It's about approaching people at the right times in their lives, when they are open for change. Most new associates will not understand that no simply means that the timing isn't right for that prospect. No doesn't mean no, it means not now. Many of the nos will end up coming into your business later and will probably join in a better position for you at that time.

When starting your business, 80 to 90 percent of your time should be spent prospecting and recruiting. Go wide! I always say, "Personally recruit until you are making what you want to make, because the best way to increase your income is to personally recruit." You are also setting the example that you want your team to follow.

Randy Hedge says, "Personal recruiting fixes all ills in your networking business." If you want a bigger team . . . personally recruit. If you want more residual income . . . personally recruit. If you want more bonus money . . . personally recruit. If you want more (fill in the blank) . . . personally recruit. Personal recruiting is the lifeblood of your business!

COACH'S SUCCESS TIP:

PERSONAL RECRUITING WILL FIX ANY PROBLEM IN YOUR NETWORK MARKETING BUSINESS.

WARM MARKET

Your warm market is made of the people you know best. They are friends, relatives, and coworkers. The reactions of friends and loved ones to our entry into network marketing can be unpredictable. Because it is unpredictable, I have found that some people do not want to talk to friends and family when they are just getting started. They will say things like, "I am just not that comfortable pitching my friends," or, "I don't want to bother my friends." These people have a BIG problem. They are not committed to network marketing or to their companies. When associates tell me they don't want to bother their friends, they are basically saying, "I do not think my business is going to be a success." You know what? If they don't change their attitude, they are right; their business will not be a success. My solution is to share with friends and family first. But I do have a few pointers as you delve into your warm list.

First, have a great attitude and expect, not hope for, the best. As with any prospect, be urgent and enthusiastic. Your excitement will be contagious.

Use the invitation skills you will learn in Chapter 11. Don't bypass setting a firm appointment for sharing all of the information just because this person is on your warm list. Resist the temptation to treat friends and family any differently than you would another person when it comes to the process. There are two reasons for this. First, the simple system is in place for a reason. Duplication lives within that simple system, so we always need to follow it, regardless of our familiarity with the person. Second, the way we approach our warm market is how they will, in turn, approach theirs, and so on. Let's not forget this is a monkey see/monkey do business.

Finally, understand that some of your warm prospects will take a wait and see attitude. They want to see how you do and whether you will stick with it. Simply put, you will experience rejection by friends and family at some point. Rest assured that it's temporary. Resist the urge to get too let down. And, more importantly, stay in the game. I can assure you that massive success will cure those feelings.

MEET NEW PEOPLE

Most of us are constantly meeting new people. We meet people at church, at school functions, while we are shopping, when our car is being worked on, at our children's sporting events, while we are eating out, when we are on vacation, or while we are walking the dog. If you don't have something in your life that is always allowing you to meet new people, find something.

The great thing about our business is that the work is simply meeting people. So, do what you love to do . . . just figure out a way to do it around more people. If you enjoy playing basketball, go to a gym and join a league. If you are an avid reader, there are tons of book clubs you could join. If you are doing what you love to do around people, it will be easy to make friends. If you are making new friends, then it will just come naturally to share what you do. Let me give you an example of this in my life.

CUCUMBER

Our son Jordan has played baseball since he was three years old. I have gone to more practices and games than I could ever count, and I have always loved it. It is what I do for fun. At these games, there are always lots of people, which is perfect for me because I am in the networking business. Here is a typical conversation for me:

"Hello. How are you? Your son is one of the best shortstops I have seen in a while. He made a heck of a diving catch a few weeks ago to save the game for you guys. That was amazing. WHAT DO YOU DO FOR A LIVING?" (This is a great question because it nearly always forces them to ask, "What do you do?")

"Oh, me? I used to be a basketball coach until I started my own business. It's been pretty lucrative, and we are expanding in this area. I tell you what: when the game is over, why don't we take the kids for hamburgers, and I can tell you more about it?"

If he's a cucumber (doesn't ask what I do or doesn't want to hear more), I just move down to the next guy.

"Howdy. Your son is the best first baseman I have seen in a while . . . WHAT DO YOU DO?"

If he is a cucumber . . .

"Howdy. Your son is the best bat boy I have ever seen."

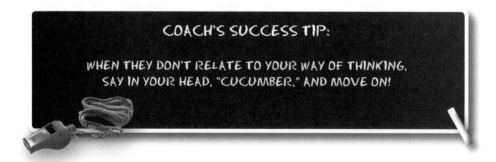

COACH'S SUCCESS TIP:

WHEN THEY DON'T RELATE TO YOUR WAY OF THINKING,
SAY IN YOUR HEAD, "CUCUMBER," AND MOVE ON!

You get the idea. It is about finding something in common so you can strike up a conversation. Make the cold market warm. As you talk and discuss the common bond, it is your chance to find out more about the other person. Ask as many questions as you can.

You will find that people love to talk about themselves. In this conversation, they usually will tell you their why if you will listen. It is easy then to position yourself as someone who may be able to help them solve their need. I have included some great questions to ask while you're bumping into people. Some of these questions are designed to start conversations, some are designed to get your prospect to open up, and some are designed to get you an appointment.

- What do you do for a living?
- Do you love what you do?
- How long have you been doing that?
- Really? Tell me a little more about that.
- How long have you lived around here?
- Tell me a little about yourself. What are your hobbies?
- Do you have children?
- What is your feeling for what the economy is going to do?
- How important do you think it is in this economy to have a plan B?
- What do you wish you had more of in your life: time or money?
- Do you ever look at other ways to make money?
- Do you keep your options open for an additional way to make money?
- Would it be okay if I showed you what I am doing to supplement my income?

If you are nervous about taking your business to people you don't know, you can practice by just talking to people while you are out. Make an effort to meet new people with no intent of sharing your opportunity. Ask them questions and learn as much as you can about them. While you are doing this, don't forget to add these new contacts to your list.

Networking is a numbers game. If you are willing to keep talking, keep setting appointments, and keep showing the plan, the cold market can be a massive pool of opportunity. Remember, strangers are just friends you haven't met yet.

I could sum up cold market prospecting with three words: make it warm. I know many people want to blast people with their opportunity, but we are and will forever be in the relationship business. The most effective way to build your business in the cold market is to make it warm. Build a relationship—or at least build some rapport—first.

Make it your goal never to run out of people on your warm market list. While getting your business started, think about ways to make new friends and build new relationships that you can begin adding to your list. Remember, prospecting and recruiting are vital to success—you need to do them every day.

HOMEWORK

1. Amateurs work from a mental list of three to five names. Professionals use a never-ending and always-growing written list of names. So it's time now for you to be a professional. It's time to create your written list of names.

2. At the top of a fresh sheet of paper, write "My List of Contacts." Make sure you write this, not type it. There is a power in writing; it's the emptying of your mind onto paper with your hand.

3. This is an important understanding to have: by physically writing down names, or emptying your mind onto paper, you're allowing your mind to fill back up with other names. So no matter what name comes to mind, quickly empty it down on paper. You do this because you know you're allowing other names to come to your conscious, out of your subconscious. Also, you'll find that one name can trigger another name. Then another. And so on.

4. On this page, List of Contacts, start writing down names. If you can only think of three names at this moment, write those three down. Just get started. Then use your cell phone. And use social media (Who is on your Facebook friends list? Who is following you on Twitter?) along with your e-mail contact list. Use the strategies from this chapter, and challenge yourself to reach one hundred names! Two hundred names? Maybe more! Push yourself, one name at a time.

Remember, your major resource in your networking business is your contacts. When you limit your list, you limit your success!

CHAPTER 10 – Seven Uses of Social Media

"The world is a magnificent place. So what are you going to do about it?"

—JIM ROHN

Social media has increased the scale and geographic reach of our relationship networks. Today, social circles have widened to encompass those with whom we maintain some degree of contact via peer networks. Social media is all about building relationships, and that's really what networking is about. Through these online communities, we can all reconnect with people we never would have had access to before. And to show you that I practice what I preach, please visit my Facebook page, www.facebook.com/presleyswagerty. Have you created your page yet? Also, check out my Twitter feed, www.twitter.com/presleyswagerty.

WINNERS EMBRACE CHANGE

Winners embrace change. Losers wish things would stay the same. As a basketball coach, I noticed that the best players were those athletes willing to work, change, adapt, and improve. Our business is no different. In the competitive game of life, entrepreneurs who embrace change have an edge over those who resist it.

Don't get me wrong: the basics will always be the basics. The fundamentals remain the fundamentals. Those never change. But certain advances, such as webinars, websites, Skype, Google+, Facebook, Twitter, Pinterest, and other social media platforms can ultimately help you and I build our businesses stronger and faster than ever before. We can't ignore these tools. My point is this: embrace change, and let's use the tools technology has given us to our advantage. If you're reluctant to accept anything new, you'll be left in the shadows while others walk on the stage!

The reason many of us resist change is that it's unfamiliar. And everything new is always unfamiliar. Each of us has a tendency to prefer the familiar and resist the unfamiliar. This is simply a part of our human nature.

To embrace change is to charge our fears head on. It's a habit we must develop. It's not something we're born with. As a math teacher for sixteen years, I found that new tools such as computers, websites, and social media initially frightened me. I was always more comfortable with a blackboard, a dusty eraser, and a thick piece of white chalk. But in studying winners, I knew that winners embrace change. I decided to step out of my comfort zone, to face the unfamiliar by educating myself on computers, websites, and social media.

My wife and kids will tell you that I have now mastered social media (kinda). It's taken a while, but through my own experiences, and by observing the thousands of associates in my organization, I feel I have a firm grasp on these tools that not too long ago frightened me. Specifically, I've learned what to do, as well as what NOT to do on social media.

The reason I've included this chapter is to guide you past the pitfalls of social media. My wish is that you use social media as the incredible tool it can be. If you'll follow my lead on this, you'll save yourself from wrecking your business and destroying your friendships, as many who have come before you have done.

It's time now to embrace change in the form of social media. Here are seven purposes for which social media should be used.

SEVEN PURPOSES OF SOCIAL MEDIA

1. Use it to get attention.
2. Use it to build trust.
3. Use it to stay in touch.
4. Use it to discover their WHYs.
5. Use it for fun and social proof.
6. Use it to get their phone number.
7. Use it to connect at a belief level.

1. USE IT TO GET ATTENTION.

Whether you know it or not, you are after the attention of people you know. Your purpose is to get their attention so you can share your business. This sounds quite simple, but it's not. You're in a constant battle against other forces that are also after their attention. Against you in this battle is all the noise that also wants their focus. Literally 800 television channels (news, sports, movies, and more) are screaming to be watched. Add to this radio, kids, spouse, dogs, cats, incoming calls, text messages, e-mails, and you can see that gaining someone's attention can be difficult! But you can overcome the noise by using social media.

Another way of saying all this is that you want to be on the front of your prospects' minds. You want them thinking of you. When they're thinking of you, you have their attention. A benefit of social media is that you can use it to gain this front-of-mind position.

A good example is when you ask a friend to look at your business. He agrees to look. But all of a sudden, he's not responsive. It's likely that you simply lost his attention; he was distracted by the noise to the point that he's not thinking about you anymore. At this point, you can use social media to regain your front position in his mind. Remember, I am NOT saying that you repeatedly message him directly or spew your business all over him with an online script. I'm simply saying that you want to be on his mind. You want his attention. And social media can help.

Make sure you do this in a positive way. Here's what I mean. You could simply post to your Twitter feed and Facebook wall: "I'm so thankful for the freedom my new business gives me!" or "I'm so happy with my new product or service!" While these are not directed specifically at any one person, you're active online and it's likely you're gaining attention. You simply want people thinking of you in a positive way. Then, once you have their attention, the next step is to keep their attention. This is where your creativity comes in. Be creative and find ways to maintain your prospects' attention on social media. Before you can share your business, you must have their attention.

2. USE IT TO BUILD TRUST.

People do business with people they know and trust. The more someone becomes familiar with you, the more he or she will trust you. Being connected on social media is a great way to build trust. By rubbing shoulders in the virtual world, the prospect becomes more familiar and comfortable with you. The level of trust begins to grow.

Furthermore, as you are open about your life to the online world via photos, comments, or interests, you'll find that more and more people will trust you. Through photos, they'll see that you are a family person. Or by your interests, they'll pleasantly discover you share similar taste in music or movies. As you open up your life, you seem more human, and the trust between you and your online following strengthens.

A final way trust is built—possibly the most powerful way—is when your prospect recognizes that the two of you share mutual friends. Having 'friends in common' is a tremendously underrated source of trust. Acquaintances will lend you trust based on their friendships with mutual friends. Social media makes all this possible.

3. USE IT TO STAY IN TOUCH.

Is it just me, or do you also find it hard to stay in touch with people? Recently, a friend of mine had a beautiful baby girl. I would never have known if social media hadn't been there to inform me. What a blessing these social media platforms can be! They allow us to stay in touch with friends and loved ones. We see where they're living and where they vacation. We see their photos in real time. We get a sense of what's going on in their lives, and it all happens with a few clicks of our mouse.

Staying in touch now only takes a matter of seconds. We can drop a quick personal note to an old high school buddy. We can comment on a funny photo posted by a long-distance relative. We can keep in touch with old coworkers. We can do many little things, but the simple act of taking the time to connect with others is what's important. This communicates to the person that we care, and that we're thinking of him or her.

Keeping in touch sounds easy enough to do. Unfortunately, as Jim Rohn says, "What's easy to do is also easy not to do." So while keeping in touch is easy to do, it's also easy not to. Decide that you're going to keep in touch. Decide that you'll initiate fresh conversations that keep you connected to friends and family.

When you operate from a heart that cares, then keeping in touch is received as genuine. Care about your friends, and this caring will draw out a desire in you to stay in touch with others on social media. You'll naturally want the best for them. Somewhere down the road, as you keep in touch, you'll discover their WHY. When that happens, you'll be positioned to help them solve their need because you cared enough to stay in touch.

4. USE IT TO DISCOVER THEIR WHYS.

God gave us two ears and one mouth so we will listen more than we speak. When we stop to listen, what do we hear? A lot of the time, I hear negativity and complaints such as, "I hate my job!" or, "I wish it were Friday!" Other times, I might hear wishful dreams, such as, "I wish I were at the beach!" or, "I need a vacation!"

Social media is a place to listen. If you'll pay close attention to the comments made by friends and family on social media, you'll often notice references to dreams, desires, or dissatisfaction. These are their WHYs—the reasons that would cause them to join your business. Whether it's in person or on a social media outlet, people will quickly reference their WHY to anyone who will listen. It's just a matter of recognizing it.

Another way of recognizing a person's WHY is to discover his or her passion. Social media can help. What does this person love? One friend of mine is a scuba diving enthusiast. You can tell by his Facebook page. So his WHY is that he wants more time and money to travel the world and scuba dive. This is a good example of using social media to discover someone's passion. Most people are looking for more free time to invest in their passions. When you discover their passions, simply connect your opportunity to their passions in some way. If family is their passion, show them how your opportunity offers more quality family time. If their church is their passion, present your opportunity as a way to benefit their church. I think you get the point. Just tinker on social media until you discover your prospects' passions. Then, position your business accordingly.

5. USE IT FOR FUN AND SOCIAL PROOF.

Everyone wants to have fun, and nobody wants to be an outsider. No one wants to miss the party! When we see others having fun, we feel drawn toward them naturally. Having fun in your business can be the glue that holds your team together. But it can also attract other friends and relatives into your endeavor. Once they see you enjoying yourself, they won't want to miss the party!

Imagine for a moment that you posted a photo of yourself online. In this photo, you're sandwiched between two of your closest networking teammates, and the three of you are arm-in-arm, smiling ear-to-ear. What does that do for your credibility? A lot, let me tell you! First, it tells your old friends and relatives that whatever it is you're up to, you're having a blast! And they don't need to hear you tell them. They can see it in the photo. Second, a photo like that is considered social proof. In essence, you're communicating indirectly to everyone, "Yes, it's socially acceptable to join my company!" All of a sudden, your old friends and relatives don't see you as that lone wolf who lost his mind. They see you having fun with others, and this warms them up to the idea of joining your team.

In networking, a big side benefit is all the new friends that you make in your business. So imagine you start adding dozens of new names to your list of online friends and online followers. These are all new friends who you're meeting at your company's events. So imagine your online following doubles in a matter of a few months! This is yet another example of social proof. Everyone on the sidelines (those who rejected your business) watch in admiration as your online popularity increases. You're using social media to show the haters that your business is indeed socially acceptable.

Showing fun and providing social proof are powerful strategies to attract people into your business. To leverage them correctly, make sure you have lots of fun, attend all the big events, take lots of fun group pictures, and post them online. You'll find that others will begin to be attracted to you and to your business. They simply don't want to miss the party!

6. USE IT TO GET THEIR PHONE NUMBERS.

I believe one of the best functions social media can offer is access to a friend's phone number.

There are no shortcuts to building a world-class organization. People may try to speed up the process by sending a mass e-mail, but what they believe is a shortcut ends in frustration and regret. Save yourself the heartache. Remember that people respond best to urgency and enthusiasm, both of which are best communicated by the texture of your voice and not by flat words on a screen. So as tempting as it might be to send a long mass e-mail, don't. You're torching your list by doing so.

Use social media to gather a person's phone number when you don't have it. Here are three messages that I might send via e-mail, text, or on social media:

- John, call me! It's important! —Presley
- Sue, e-mail me your phone number ASAP, thanks! —Presley
- Pete, what's your cell number? —Presley

I keep it very simple. All I want is to get that person on the phone. On the phone is where I'll set the appointment. On the phone is where he or she will hear my excitement and feel my enthusiasm. On the phone! So use social media to get their phone numbers, and then pick up the phone and call the person.

7. USE IT TO CONNECT ON A BELIEF LEVEL.

A friend was watching the local news as we sat in an unfamiliar restaurant. On the television, the talking heads were taking turns bashing the president over foreign policy. My friend, who was captivated by this, opened his mouth and said a few comments indicating that he, too, believed the president was in the wrong. To my amazement, our waitress spun around and chimed right in. She enthusiastically agreed. And then she proceeded to enter into a conversation with my buddy. It seemed two strangers just became instant best friends. This was incredible because just moments before, our waitress had acted cold and distant to us. But that all changed when she heard my friend speak. It was my friend's and her mutual beliefs, connecting on a deeper level that caused this transformation.

A similar occurrence happened recently. I'm a Dallas Cowboys fan, and I was wearing a Cowboys T-shirt, walking through enemy territory: the Philadelphia airport. Surprisingly, I happened to notice a complete stranger wearing a Cowboys ball cap, coming from the opposite direction. He quickly noticed my Cowboys T-shirt and we immediately struck up a friendly conversation. It was as though we were good friends, even though we were complete strangers! The reason: we connected on a belief level.

Beliefs are strong opinions. They're seated in our character. We own our beliefs. And when we connect with someone on a belief level, something magical occurs. We feel like family. We feel like longtime friends. It's important that you're aware of the power of beliefs. They can bring a strong connection to you and someone else, especially on social media.

But the reverse can happen as well. It's equally as possible for beliefs to become a brick wall separating you from people in your pool of contacts. For example, imagine that you're online when a close friend makes the brash comment, "All non-Republicans should leave Texas!" And what if you're not a Republican? Instantly, your friend just became less of a friend. There's a feeling of separation now. A wall went up. You're disconnected at a belief level. So be careful in what you say on social media.

The good news is that you can use beliefs to connect with people whom you hardly know. Let's say that you post "I believe baseball is the greatest sport on earth!" You obviously will attract and connect with other baseball enthusiasts. Or, if you said, "Brad Paisley is the best guitarist ever!" There's no doubt that other Brad Paisley fans would feel a stronger connection with you. I can go on and on with examples. Just understand: beliefs are strong forces that can build relation-ships or tear them apart. You can be instant friends with strangers once they find out you share the same beliefs.

In closing, just be careful that you don't disconnect yourself by care-lessly blasting your beliefs onto social media. You're building your business. You're building your future. You can't afford to be casual with what you say. Always share your beliefs in a way that builds stronger bonds with those you'd like to share your business.

HOMEWORK

Below are a few questions to help you pull the most from this chapter. Grab a pen and paper and write down your answers. The questions are a natural progression into the Action Steps that follow.

1. Decide today that you will be an expert in the use of social media. Decide that you will drop all excuses. Decide that you will master this realm and that other leaders will come to you for knowledge in this area.

2. Who are three people in your life who know the absolute most about social media? They might be eight years old, or they might be eighty years old. Reach out and ask them to teach you about social media. Speed up your learning curve by observing these people.

3. Create a Facebook page or, if you already have one, update it and make it part of your network marketing business plan. How can you use your Facebook site to stay in touch? Drum up business? Connect on a belief level?

4. Start Tweeting! Are you on Twitter? Follow Coach @presleyswagerty and create your own account so you can share every time you meet a goal or have other good news.

5. Visit Coach's website, www.presleyswagerty.com, and explore a little. Now, start building your own website, if you don't already have one.

6. Who are five to ten neglected friends on social media with whom you should reconnect immediately to begin rebuilding a bond?

7. Every day, reach out to two people on social media without prospecting them for your business. In other words, every day, take a sincere interest into the lives of two people. You might compliment their pictures; you might comment on their posts. You might applaud them in some way, or ask how they're doing. You might highlight commonalities. You might just say hello. The idea here is to get outside of yourself and habitually practice caring for, and thinking about, other people. This practice alone, doing it consistently every day, will do wonders for your online relationships.

CHAPTER 11 – Four Steps to Setting Appointments

"Leave nothing for tomorrow which can be done today."

—ABRAHAM LINCOLN

I love Abraham Lincoln's quote, even though it doesn't directly apply to appointment setting. I included it because if you are anything like me, you put off picking up the phone to set appointments. I hope this chapter gives you the confidence to start making those calls today.

Learning how to set appointments is critical to your success. Appointment setting is most often done by phone. Your primary objective is to set appointments with the people on your list, so you can show them a business presentation. If you're not getting in front of people, then your business isn't growing.

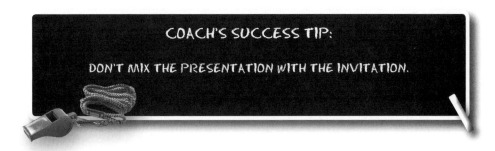

COACH'S SUCCESS TIP:

DON'T MIX THE PRESENTATION WITH THE INVITATION.

The biggest mistake new associates usually make is saying too much when inviting someone to see a presentation. The sole purpose of the invitation is to set an appointment—not to explain the business. That will come during the presentation. Trying to show a presentation over the phone is like trying to give someone a haircut over the phone. It can't be done. When mixing the presentation with the invitation, you will fall into what I call the valley of death. It's hard to get out once you find yourself there. Make sure to keep the invitation separate from the presentation. Focus on setting the appointment and staying out of the valley of death, and your appointments will increase dramatically.

The best approach to invite someone to see your opportunity is a direct one. I use the Four Circle Method created by an amazing networker named Chris LaFaive. Consider the following illustration:

THE FOUR CIRCLE METHOD

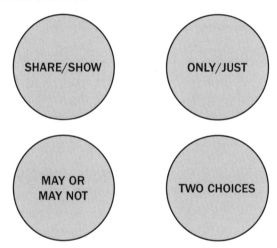

- Use all Four Circles
- Circles can be used in any order
- Be enthusiastic
- Have a strong voice or tone while setting the appointment

Here is why the Four Circles work so well.

Share/Show

The Share/Show circle is where you can tailor the invitation to the person with whom you are setting an appointment. If the person is a businessperson, try, "I have a business deal I want to show you." If he or she is a stay-at-home parent, say, "I have some information that was shared with me and that I want to share with you."

Only/Just

The Only/Just circle lets your prospect know that you are not after a lot of his or her time. It doesn't matter how much time you need, always say only or just. Try, "I only need twenty minutes."

May or May Not

The May or May Not circle is very important. This is the part of the invitation that lets people know it is okay if they are not interested. It makes them feel comfortable that you will not try to twist their arms to get them into your business. The correct use of this circle allows you to be pushy about getting the appointment because you can emphasize that you will NOT be pushy once you are sitting down with them. Say, "You may or may not be interested, but I have something I'd like to share with you."

Two Choices

The most important circle is Two Choices. This circle is the single greatest appointment-setting skill to learn. If you ask a child, "Would you like vegetables for dinner?" he usually responds, "No." If you ask an adult, "Would you like to come to an opportunity meeting?" she usually responds, "No." On the other hand, many mothers have learned that a child likes to choose: "What vegetable would you like for dinner tonight—peas or carrots?" The child jumps at the opportunity to make a choice. Adults are the same. We all want to be in control, so this allows us to pass control back to the prospect. "What day works best for you this week, John, Tuesday or Wednesday?" If it is a particularly tough prospect to nail down, start very general with your choices: "What generally works best for you, John? Weekends or weekdays?" From there, start narrowing the choices, "Okay, which day on the weekend is better typically, Saturday or Sunday?" "Do you usually have more free time in the morning or in the afternoon on Saturdays?"

HANDLING OBJECTIONS WHEN SETTING APPOINTMENTS

Many people will be anxious to hear about your business opportunity, but you will also encounter a few skeptics. The person you have approached for an appointment may raise an objection such as, "I don't have the money," or, "I'm too busy," or, "I'm not a salesperson." Most objections are well intentioned, but are little more than excuses in disguise. The most effective response to every objection when trying to set an appointment is, "You won't hurt my feelings if you don't want to get involved, but at least take a look. Does Tuesday or Wednesday work better?"

How can anyone say NO if he or she doesn't KNOW? Remember, your objective is to set an appointment. You simply want an opportunity to share 100 percent of the information. The key is your strong belief that no one can make a decision until he or she has seen a presentation.

COACH'S SUCCESS TIP:

HOW CAN ANYONE SAY NO . . . IF HE OR SHE DOESN'T KNOW?

Here are some examples of the Four Circle Method:

Joe,
I've got something I want to share with you. You may or may not be interested. I only need 20 minutes. Does Tuesday or Wednesday work better?

Sue,
You may or may not be interested, but I have something I want to show you. It will only take 20 minutes; does Monday or Wednesday work better?

Raul,
I only need 30 minutes to show you something. You may or may not be interested. Does Thursday or Friday work better for you?

Betty,
Does Tuesday morning or Wednesday afternoon work better for you? I've got something I want to share with you. You may or may not be interested, but it will only take 20 minutes.

If the appointment does not get set in the first pass, don't panic. If the prospect asks for more information or asks, "Can you tell me a little more about it?" Answer, "Yes!" or, "Absolutely!"

Here are two options when the prospect says, "Can you tell me more about it?"

Option A

"Can you tell me more about it?"

Answer with a third-party credibility piece or award: "Yes, of course . . . the company I am working with recently won the XYZ award for customer excellence." Then go right back to the four circles. This time, put an emphasis on the "may or may not be interested" circle and the "only/just" circle.

Option B

"Can you tell me more about it?"

"Yes, I would love to. Do you have twenty minutes right now?" Be prepared to go to her and show the business or to do a web presentation. Most of the time, this will usually end in a "No" response from your prospect. Go back to the four circles and emphasize that you really need the twenty minutes to tell her more about it.

Often people will want to know what it is and start asking questions. When they ask for details, I tell them, "It's a visual deal. I need to sit down with you and show you some numbers. Does Tuesday or Wednesday work better?"

ENTHUSIASM AND URGENCY

I lovingly refer to my friend Susan Fisher as "Ignorance on Fire." When she joined our company, she had no clue how the compensation plan worked. She had no idea how anything worked. I doubt she could have told you the name of our company! But none of that mattered. Why? Because she was so excited, and that made up for her lack of knowledge! When Susan walked into the room, you could feel her presence. She moved with urgency. You could feel her enthusiasm. Today, Susan has earned millions of dollars in networking. She's a top producer, and she's inspired thousands of people. Along the way, Susan has taught me a lesson: enthusiasm and urgency are more important than knowledge.

What you say is not as important as how you say it. People may hear what you say but—more important— they feel how you say it. Enthusiasm is your greatest asset. If you are excited, it's natural for your excitement to transfer to the person you are talking to. The flip side is certainly true, too, though: if you're not excited, it's virtually impossible for your prospect to get excited. It's that simple.

Urgency is a natural byproduct of enthusiasm. If your opportunity is important and you're excited about your new business, then you'll come across with urgency in your invitation. "How soon?" are two fantastic words you can use to communicate urgency. For example, "John, how soon can you and I get together?"

THE AS-IF PRINCIPLE

"But Presley, what if I don't feel excited?" Good question! After all, we're human, and our emotions change on a daily or even hourly basis. What if you wake up and you're not excited? What do you do then? Here's the key: Your emotions dictate your actions. But . . . your actions can also dictate your emotions! Use the as-if principle. Act as if you are excited. If you act excited, you'll soon feel excited. So act excited! Act with urgency! As a result, you will soon feel swept away by the feeling of enthusiasm that you're looking for. Your feelings will ultimately catch up and mirror your actions.

Use your enthusiasm to get everyone you know to see a business presentation, and your opportunity will sell itself, just as it did for you. Every phone call you make, every appointment you set, and every conversation you take part in—have a sense of urgency.

HOMEWORK

For this homework assignment, you will need a partner, someone to help you in person or over the phone. If you're married, your spouse can fill this role. Otherwise, I recommend you call your sponsor, a team leader, or anyone else in your chosen business to help you in this exercise.

One of the top five reasons people fail in network marketing is that they don't practice. In other words, they don't role-play. As a coach, I think it would be absurd to consider playing in a competitive basketball game without practicing first. Similarly, it's crazy to consider making a phone call for your business without role-playing before the call. Role-playing is practicing for networking.

1. Turn back to the page that has the Four Circles. With your partner, role-play a phone call using the Four Circles.

2. Then role-play it again and again and again. Each time, use the Four Circles in a different order and show lots of enthusiasm.

3. Continue to do this until you become fully comfortable with the Four Circles and how they interact with each other. The idea is that you get so good that you don't need to look at the Four Circles. It becomes second nature. And when it's natural, that's when you know you're ready for the game.

Note: It's important after you role-play that you start making actual calls. Practice, by itself, doesn't pay the mortgage or create financial freedom. So immediately after you role-play, make a real call, then another, then another. Once you're in motion, you'll find it easy to stay in motion.

By the way, it's okay to have some fun. Make sure you have a few good laughs as you role-play the calls. Be serious about getting it right, but have some fun along the way.

CHAPTER 12 – Have Fun with 1-on-1s and 2-on-1s

SHOWING THE PLAN

In networking, there are only two activities that really count: showing the business presentation and selling your products or services. That's it. Period. If we are not showing the plan to other people or gathering customers then we are not working the business. In this profession, the associate that shows the most business presentations wins!

There are several ways to present the business opportunity to your prospects. Your sponsor or upline should always be enlisted to help you with your first few presentations. However, the sooner you learn to do a business presentation yourself, the sooner your business will explode. Let's start with 1-on-1s and 2-on-1s.

1-ON-1 BUSINESS PRESENTATION

I love 1-on-1s and 2-on-1s, and I built a lot of my business using them. You don't have to be an expert to make your initial 1-on-1 presentation. You actually don't want to be too polished; just state the facts with enthusiasm.

Try to choose a coffee shop or a restaurant that is convenient for the prospect, and do your 1-on-1 presentations in 30 minutes or less so your prospect can see that business presentations can be done quickly.

I recommend that you don't do high-pressure business presentations. Simply share your information and, when you're finished, ask your prospect to join your team. You must always ask them to join. Use your ABCs . . . Always Be Closing.

Remember, if they don't want to join your team, get them as your customer.

During the business presentation, speak to the prospect as if he or she is already in. Talk about him or her building a team, making money, and changing his or her life.

When doing 1-on-1 presentations, you've got to be flexible about the location. I've done 1-on-1 presentations in barber shops and in beauty shops. I've done presentations at the gym. I've done presentations in the parking lot at church. I've done presentations on the hood of a car. I've done presentations under shade trees. I've done presentations in grocery stores. I've done presentations at the hunting lease. I've done presentations at a pawnshop. I remember one time I walked into a pawnshop—the owner was sitting behind bars and a couple of Doberman Pinschers were growling at me—and I did the presentation through the bars with him on one side and me on the other.

It's not always at a coffee shop or a restaurant. You have to be flexible and take the presentation to your prospect.

1-ON-1 PRESENTATIONS

Advantages

- Convenient.

- Personal.

Disadvantages

- You are not an expert to your friend.

- You may not be profitable yet.

1-on-1 Business Presentation Guidelines:

- Arrive early to get a good spot.

- Pick the quietest spot possible.

- Use a tool to show the presentation . . . preferably a video.

- Talk about the great team that you are a part of, and show pictures, if possible.

- Incorporate a three-way phone call with someone who is successful in your company.

- Be enthusiastic.

It is very important for you to understand that whatever you do, your prospects will think they have to do. It is okay not to know the answer to every question; this shows your friend that it is okay not to understand every detail. More importantly, show prospects that you know how to get the answer. This is a great time to incorporate a three-way call.

THREE-WAY CALL

The three-way call is a great way to leverage the knowledge and success of your sponsor and upline leaders. You can call them at the end of a presentation to share a testimonial with your prospect or to answer questions. Remember, your prospects are usually people who know you. This allows a third-party "expert" to share insight about the business with your prospect, who may not see you as an expert since he or she knows you are just getting started in networking. In short, the three-way call is a great option when you are showing the plan either in person or online and you want an outside expert to seal the deal.

2-ON-1 BUSINESS PRESENTATIONS

When you are new to networking, you are usually not a good advertisement for your opportunity. You haven't made much money, you probably have a negative cash flow, and you don't know a lot of the answers. What can you do? Find a successful person in your upline chain of leadership who is willing to mentor you and help you with 2-on-1 business presentations. Take this person to the presentation with you and watch him or her in action. In traditional businesses, employees are hesitant to ask someone to act as a mentor. They worry that busy, successful people will have no time for them. But in networking, your upline leaders have a financial interest in helping you.

2-ON-1 PRESENTATIONS

Advantages:

- Convenient.

- Power of third-party credibility.

- Duplicable.

- An experienced third-party expert can answer difficult questions.

Disadvantages:

- You are bringing a stranger.

2-on-1 Business Presentation Guidelines:

- Set the appointment with the prospect, and then coordinate with the upline leader. Reschedule with the prospect if need be.

- It is best to tell the prospect while setting the appointment that you will be bringing your business partner or friend with you to the appointment.

- Arrive early to get a good spot.

- Pick the quietest spot possible.

- Edify the leader you bring as being an expert in your industry and describe his or her success.

- Stay fully engaged during the presentation.

- Once you turn it over to your upline leader, do not speak unless your leader asks for your input directly.

TAKE AN ACTIVE ROLE

I tell people all the time that you want to get lost in the success of your downline if you want to have success. Zig Ziglar tells us, "If you help enough other people get what they want, then you can have anything that you want."

When you sign somebody up, you don't just say, "Hey, go do it—go make me rich." You have to take an active role with the people you sponsor; take responsibility for their success.

STORY OF DEANO AND FLO

Here is a story that illustrates this point. Mark Dean sold us a car for SaraBeth. During the car-buying process, I asked him if he had looked at other ways to make money and he said yes. I set an appointment to meet him the next day for lunch at Jason's Deli, showed him our business, and he decided to join the team. When I finished signing Deano up, I asked him, "Are you free tomorrow? Can you meet at Starbucks on North Garland Avenue in the morning at 9:00?"

He said, "Yeah."

So, on Saturday morning, we met at Starbucks and got a latte.

I said, "Let's go get in the car." We got in my car. I looked at Deano and said, "Who's somebody we can go show this to?"

It was kind of funny because he wasn't expecting that. Deano's eyes got real big. He said, "What do you mean?"

I said, "Well, in this business, the way you make money is you set appointments and show the plan. We've got to get the presentation in front of some people. Who can we go show?"

He said, "Well, I've got a sister."

I said, "Well, call your sister."

Deano got his cell phone and called his sister. She was available, so we went to her house and showed her the presentation. She didn't get in.

We got back in the car. I was a little disappointed, but I never showed it to Deano. I said, "Okay, who else can we go talk to?"

Deano looked at me and replied, "Well, I've got another sister."

I said, "Great, let's call your other sister."

We sat at the table at Denny's and signed Flo up. As we're getting ready to leave, it hit me. I looked at Flo and said, "What are you doing the rest of the afternoon? You busy?"

She said, "Nah, I'm pretty flexible."

I said, "Why don't you go with us?"

I put Deano in the back seat and Flo in the front seat. I did Flo the same way I did Deano. I looked at her and I said, "Who can we go show this to?"

She said, "I've got a brother."

We went and showed Flo's brother at a printing facility. Big machines were going all around us, and I showed the presentation on a little rickety table. I had to shout because the noise was so loud.

The whole point is that I got Deano in, said, "Let's go," and we started showing the plan, doing 2-on-1s. If I had told him to go do it, it may never have gotten done. Today, Deano and Flo are Top 10 money earners who have made millions of dollars. Take an active role with your team, and it will pay big dividends.

HOMEWORK

1. Get your prospect list out and schedule four or five 1-on-1s or 2-on-1s.

2. When someone signs up, take the same approach that I did with Deano: put the new associate in the car and start showing the plan to people he or she knows. We learn by doing, so get started.

3. Tweet or post to Facebook your goal to schedule some meetings.

CHAPTER 13 – Awesome Home and Hotel Events

HOME EVENTS

Another great way to get your business going is to host a home event. Home events are informal get-togethers, during which you invite your prospects to see a business presentation at your home. They are easy to do and a friendly, non-threatening way for prospects to see your business.

TIM ROSE'S HOME EVENT

Reflecting on home events reminds me of a buddy of mine, Tim Rose. Tim lived in Tyler, Texas, in the eastern part of the state. I live in the Dallas area, and Tyler is about two hours away.

Tim was excited to get his business going so I said, "Why don't you invite a few folks over to your house, and I will come and do a home event for you?"

That is exactly what Tim did. So I drove a couple of hours to get to Tim's house, we shared the opportunity with a few people, and two of them joined our team.

I drove back home that night and got home around midnight. I remember getting a call the next day. Tim asked, "Hey, Presley, could you do another presentation tomorrow night?"

"Absolutely, Tim."

So, I drove back to East Texas. We met a few more people in Tim's living room. The ones who got in at the previous meeting also brought a few folks so the event got a little bigger. We showed the presentation, and a few more people joined our business.

I got home again about midnight, but our success made me feel good about doing the business. It was working. A couple of days later, Tim called again and said, "Can we do another home event?"

"Sure, Tim."

I drove back to Tyler, and that meeting was even bigger. Tim invited a few more, and the people who got in the previous two events invited a few.

We got Tim's business off and running by doing several home events. Home events are very laid back; they're casual and non-threatening. They are a great way to get your business jump-started at a fast pace. Home events can lay the foundation for success.

Tim is now a top money earner in our company. It all started with just a few home events in Tyler, Texas.

HOME EVENTS

Advantages:

- Non-threatening.

- Social.

- Team oriented.

- Warm and casual for the guests.

Disadvantages:

- Guests are sometimes suspicious of network marketing.

- Must have advanced planning.

- More preparation than other methods.

Home Event Guidelines:

- Call your guests enough in advance to allow them to plan their schedule.

- Have two choices when setting the appointment for your prospect.

- Don't be afraid to invite more than your home can accommodate. There will be the inevitable no-shows. A packed house is a good thing. You can even present twice, back-to-back, if necessary.

- Make sure that your home is clean and presentable.

- Start on time and keep the event short. Respect the allotted time. Finish within the time frame you promised your guests.
- Prepare minor refreshments . . . NOT A MEAL. Drinks are fine, but no food or alcohol. Bottled water is a great choice.
- Eliminate distractions such as televisions, dogs, and phones.
- Keep the entire meeting duplicable. Show an opportunity video if possible. Use your company's DVD presentation, or have one of the more experienced associates do the presentation.
- If appropriate, have another associate provide a brief testimonial.
- The host should welcome everyone and edify the presenter.
- Help new associates schedule their own home meetings.
- Make sure prospects know that there is going to be a business presentation. Don't try to trick people. Be up front with your prospects.

THE BAG OF ICE TECHNIQUE

Most times, people will ask if they can bring something. If you are really worried about someone's not showing up, tell the person that you have all the refreshments taken care of; but, if they would bring the ice, it would be a huge help. You may end up with a couple of bags of ice in your freezer, but you will be amazed at how less often people stand you up. If they are going to no-show, they will usually call in advance.

COACH'S SUCCESS TIP:

USE THE BAG OF ICE TECHNIQUE!

HOTEL EVENTS

Hotel events are great, but I believe hotel events are for the associates more than for the prospects. Hotel events are when you rally your team. Don't get me wrong;

if you can get a guest to a hotel event, that's awesome, but hotel events are my least favorite first-look method. Home events, 1-on-1s, and 2-on-1s are my favorites. Hotel events are great for a second look or for reinforcement.

When inviting someone to a hotel event, put the person in your car when possible, and take him or her to the event. If you can't take the person, have him or her meet you at a nearby restaurant or coffee shop before the event. That way your prospects know you are showing up for them.

Share photos and details of fun, high energy hotel events on your Twitter and Facebook, using #CoachPresley.

When the company I'm involved with began to expand nationally, our first expansion was Georgia. Georgia was amazing—not just in the explosion our business experienced right from the launch, but in the many friends and leaders we have come to know through our Georgia expansion. One couple personifies the power of the hotel event. Their names are Jon and Tammy Nowicki. To understand the impact hotel events had on their lives and business, you have to hear their story.

EVOLUTION OF A HOTEL MEETING

When we first started our network marketing journey in May of 2008, we partnered with Bob and Melinda Nash and Mike Hubbard to see whether we could get something started in our area. The company was launching Georgia as the first state on the highly anticipated national expansion, and we wanted to take advantage of the excitement and huge opportunity. Because the company would be new to Georgia, we all got together and decided to talk to everyone we knew. We also wanted to provide a place where people could come to learn more after their first introduction to the venture.

Moreover, we anticipated that prospective business partners would want to know that they were going to have some help. Nobody wants to start something and feel like he or she is all alone. Our goal was to create a team environment in which people could have a place to come to get their questions answered. We first committed to doing a weekly business presentation in a small conference room that Mike Hubbard had at his business. The room would hold about twenty people comfortably, and we set up a laptop/projector to show the PowerPoint presentation.

Our goal starting out was to present our business in a professional, but low-pressure (nonthreatening) environment. We all committed to one day a week, when at least one of us would be available to show the business presentation and teach/train the people who wanted to get started afterward. We didn't expect big numbers, especially since we were heading into summer, but we committed to every Wednesday. In retrospect, a huge key to our success was the commitment we made from the very start. We all committed to being there whether or not anyone showed up.

Now, this may sound comical, but our first problem in presenting the business was that none of us knew anything about it! Enter our sponsor, Becky Bigbie.

Becky knew she needed to come to Georgia to help us at the beginning, but she ended up going above and beyond, flying out about once a month for the first six months. Becky is a top earner in the business, and she knew what we needed.

Initially, she trained us on how to do the business presentation and then answered a ton of questions for us over the phone. We kept Mike's conference room set up during the day, and it was common for us to meet prospects daily and then direct them to a second exposure, the Wednesday night business presentation. Attendance was sparse at first, but we were soon filling the room as a few told a few. The defining moment came when Becky and top-five money earner Greg McCord came out to speak. With not one, but two, mega-successful networkers, it was standing-room only! We probably had forty to fifty people packed in that small and very hot room. It was then that we decided to move to a bigger facility. Becky was supportive of the idea and willing to help finance a move to a local hotel. We started brainstorming how to run a great hotel event.

- Becky felt she could line up a steady stream of top leaders as guest speakers.
- We found a great, high-quality host hotel.
- Mike came up with fantastic audio/visual equipment.
- We made sure our Business Plan was exactly by the standards set by corporate.

- We got a commitment from our team to make Wednesday night a priority.
- We set up greeters and a sign-in table every week.
- Tammy became great at using e-mail reminders to promote the meeting/ speakers.
- We did trainings in addition to the BP.
- After the meeting, we hung around to socialize and then met at a local restaurant for our team "sizzle session."

As our events started at the hotel, Becky did exactly as she had said she would, and she brought in a top money earner as a guest speaker almost every week. We quickly realized how powerful everyone's story was, and we started to promote the speakers' stories from week to week. The promotion of the events became a huge key. We couldn't just expect people to show up; we had to give them a reason to want to come.

The initial room we had at the hotel quickly filled up. We had them move us to their amphitheater room to accommodate all the guests. The amazing amphitheater fueled the fire, and the momentum really took off about two months in. It culminated with the appearance of the author of this book and our company's number-one earner, Presley Swagerty.

We had been regularly filling the amphitheater when other top money earners spoke; but with Presley we had to bring in extra chairs for the floor area, and we had people sitting on the steps!

We initially set out to start something in our little area of Georgia, but an amazing thing happened along the way. Not only did our team explode and grow beyond our wildest dreams, but the hotel event we started also took on a life all its own. Through that amazing phenomenon, our hotel event became an integral key to growing many other teams across the state and across the country, as well. We were just blessed to be part of it.

—Jon and Tammy Nowicki

I think you'll agree that Jon and Tammy have created an awesome weekly event. I like to think of every opportunity meeting as an event. It is your chance to showcase so much more than your compensation plan.

COACH'S SUCCESS TIP:

PROMOTE TOP EARNER AND GUEST SPEAKER APPEARANCES BY SHARING THEIR STORIES IN TEAM CONFERENCE CALLS AND CORRESPONDENCE LEADING UP TO THE EVENT.

TIPS FOR A GREAT HOTEL EVENT

As guests enter the room for the first time, they take into account everything that is going on. They make judgments based on how people are dressed, how others act, and even how the room itself appears. Here are a few tips that will help you have great success at your weekly meeting.

ARRIVE EARLY

It is important to arrive a few minutes early because in networking, everything we do is observed. You can tell a guest anything you want, but if he or she does not see it in your actions, that guest will not believe you. It is the old adage: practice what you preach. Arriving early shows your guests that you are excited about what is going on. It also shows them that you are serious about your business. Imagine that you had an important real estate meeting with Donald Trump, and you showed up ten minutes after the scheduled start time. None of us would ever be so careless. At our events, the top earners and leaders take time out of their schedules to help us build our businesses. Treat it like a million-dollar business meeting, and you will potentially build a million-dollar business.

HAVE FUN

If we all follow the first rule, then our guests will arrive at the event and see a room full of people. But do those people look like people with whom we want to associate? Do you remember the old Head and Shoulders slogan, "Because you never get a second chance to make a first impression"? People already have jobs and don't want another one. The beauty of a networking business is that it can be fun. It is a social business where we are paid to talk and socialize with people. Have you ever asked people why they like their job and they answer, "Because it is a serious place to work"? No. They answer, "It is a fun place to work." Our business should be fun. Our events should be fun. Making money is fun. Let's act like it!

CARE ABOUT THE DETAILS

The details are what allow us to have a fun atmosphere while maintaining a professional feel. The details range from the way the leaders dress to the audio quality.

What most people do not realize is that many things go on behind the scenes to transform an average event into a great event. If you get there early, ask yourself, "What can I do to make this room better?" It may mean rearranging the chairs a little or adjusting the projector so the image is straight. Sometimes the temperature is uncomfortable; ask a few other attendees to make sure, and then find a worker who can adjust the room temperature. If the room is going to be hard to find, ask a few volunteers to help direct people to the right place. Work with the other attendees to brainstorm about ways to make your event better. Always consult with the top-ranking associate at your meeting for his or her counsel before implementing a new idea.

COACH'S SUCCESS TIP:

IT'S THE LITTLE THINGS THAT MAKE THE BIG THINGS WORK.

SENDING A GUEST

Sometimes you will have someone that you want to share your business opportunity with, and who does not live close enough for you to go to an event together. There is no real replacement for your being with your prospect at the first look. However, if you must have him or her attend an event without you, there are a few things you can do to make it the best possible experience.

First, find the closest event to your prospect. Often, your company will list events on its website, and you can determine who runs the event close to your prospect. If you can't find out who runs the event, talk to leaders and find out. When you find a contact person, call him to introduce yourself and let him know that you have a guest who may attend the event. Ask him to tell you a little about the event: How many attend? Who usually presents? Does he know of any special guest planning to be there? Ask him if it is okay for your guest to introduce himself and whether the contact person is willing to help answer any questions your prospect may have.

Next, call your prospect and set a firm appointment for him to attend the event. Let him know a little about what to expect at the event. Give him the address and directions to the location. Tell him a little about the person you spoke with on the phone. Edify the host; let your prospect know he is going to meet someone who is having great success in the business.

Finally, the day of the meeting, confirm with your guest and make sure he is still able to attend. Ask him to call you on his way home after the meeting so you can discuss the opportunity. It is your job—not anyone's at the meeting—to follow up.

Obviously, we would all choose to be sitting right next to our guest at the event. If, however, you are unable to attend, follow these guidelines, and your guest should have a great experience.

HOTEL EVENTS

Advantages:
- Top leaders as presenters.
- Power in numbers.
- Guest sees the culture of your company.
- Guest meets people with similar backgrounds.

Disadvantages:
- May not be convenient.

Hotel Event Guidelines:
- Depending on the popularity of the meeting, arrive 15–30 minutes early.
- If possible, pick your guest up and drive him.
- Before the presentation, introduce your guest to other leaders.
- After the presentation, introduce your guest to each presenter.
- Sit on the front row. (I call this millionaire row.)

HOMEWORK

1. Here it is: host a home event. That's it. Simple. But will you do it? If your own home can't accommodate people, ask a friend or family member if you can use his or her home (a great strategy to make sure that person will be in attendance). Once you've scheduled this home event, invite your sponsor and your team leaders. Then, of course, invite your guests. Consider yourself the promoter for this event. Your role is to put butts in seats! The more people, the better. Having too many people is a good problem to have.

2. The key is to take immediate action and schedule your initial home event now. Next, follow this up by setting a second home event, then a third. This allows your guests to invite their guests the following time. Even if it starts with just one person, that's a start. Go from there. Build it to two people, then to four people. It's like starting with a penny: keep doubling it, and soon you will have a fortune! The key is to start with that first penny. That first home event with that first guest. Important note: Your enthusiasm, more than anything else, will get them in the seats and then into your business.

3. Now go ahead, grab your calendar, and pick the day. Schedule your first home event, and you'll be on your way. Tweet your plans and post the event to your Facebook wall and your website.

CHAPTER 14 – Websites and Webinars

As technology expands and improves, websites and webinars are now a great way to share your business. When I think of using a company website as a presentation tool, I think of top-earner Ajax Daugherty. Ajax is from Dallas and has a heart as big as Texas. To reach out and help his associates and prospects in the far reaches of Texas and other states, Ajax has become a master at what he likes to call the First Look. You see, Ajax doesn't believe in just blasting a mass e-mail with a link to a website. On the contrary, he's developed an awesome technique that has served his team well. Now don't misunderstand, Ajax and I are both believers that face-to-face is best; but when face-to-face is not possible, or when time is of the essence, there is no better alternative than Ajax's method. Here's what Ajax had to share about the First Look.

> ## FIRST LOOK WEBSITE PRESENTATIONS
>
> The goal of the First Look is to explain the business opportunity to the candidate using your website business presentation video and a third-party expert. The secret is demonstrating the urgency and enthusiasm both you and the third-party expert share for the program. Here's how it is done:

1. **Choose a third-party expert.** The expert can be your sponsor or one of your upline leaders, anyone who is not you. While financial success in the business is certainly a good thing, it isn't a prerequisite to being the expert in this scenario. Expert, when it comes to the First Look, is more of a role than a descriptive term. Remember, your prospects don't know you as a networking expert, so they will respond better to having their questions answered by a stranger who has been edified as an expert.

2. **Orient the third-party expert to the prospect.** For the expert to develop rapport with your prospect, the expert needs you to give him or her an advance thumbnail sketch of the prospect. For example, share useful information that may include the prospect's age group, hobbies, interests, family status, potential reasons why the prospect may see network marketing as an option, and so on. This will help your expert keep his or her role concise and on task. Remember; be the messenger and NOT the message. Leave that to the expert!

3. **Make the call, and edify the expert.** After your expert has the thumbnail sketch, make the call. Your job is simply to make the introduction. It is imperative that you edify the third-party expert as the expert . . . a person who is going places.

4. **Build rapport.** The third-party expert will then build rapport with the prospect. Hold rapport building down to three to five minutes before the presentation.

5. **Prepare the prospect for the business presentation.** The expert asks the prospect to have a piece of paper in front of her, with a line drawn down the middle. While watching the website video presentation, instruct the prospect to do two things:
   a. Write down questions that come to mind on the left-hand side.
   b. Write down people who come to mind on the right-hand side.

6. **Instruct the prospect to view the business presentation via the website video.** Let her know exactly how long the video runs and that you will call back in exactly that amount of time to answer her questions. Remind her once more to write down questions and names on the paper in front of her. Ask her to click play on the presentation, and then you hang up.

7. **Make a follow-up call.** Call back exactly at the promised time. First, ask her if she was able to see the entire presentation. If she was interrupted, offer to remain on the line while she finishes. If she completed the video, say, "Great. How many names did you write down?" After she responds, make note of the answer, and then say, "Let's answer your questions first. How many do you have?"

8. **Lots of names and some questions.** Names and no questions are great indicators of interest. Ask her to share her questions beginning with the one most important to her. Answer the questions. Then say, "How would you like your name to appear on your checks?" Begin the enrollment.

9. **No names and no questions.** No names and no questions leave us unsure as to the interest level of the prospect. I'd say, "What do you like best about our business venture?" Proceed based on the level of interest indicated.

10. **Few names and questions.** This indicates interest, but the level of interest is still to be determined. In this example, I like to ask the prospect which of her questions is most critical to establishing her level of interest. I then say, "If I can answer that question to your satisfaction, is there any reason why you wouldn't like to get started today?" If she replies no, answer the question satisfactorily and begin the enrollment. If I can tell the time is not right in the prospect's life, I simply help her become my customer and move her to my follow-up list.

Now you may be wondering why I am such a proponent of the First Look. It's simple. The First Look is a success tool, and simply put, it's the next best thing to being there! Just look at some of the examples of my team's First Look success stories.

I had an attorney in Pennsylvania, introduced to our business via an associate on my team from Virginia. Bob was fifty-eight years old and practicing law. With two daughters in out-of-state, private colleges, additional income was a topic that appealed to him. However, he had his legal reputation to protect and his personal reputation to maintain. Bob needed credible reassurance to that end. I had gathered this information from my thumbnail sketch that I get prior to the First Look. With the thumbnail sketch in hand, I contacted a top earner from our company, Kirk Newsom, a practicing attorney in Dallas, and arranged for him to be on the call with me. It just made sense for another attorney to address Bob's concerns. We created rapport with Bob quickly and effortlessly with the career connection and walked him through the First Look. Bob now holds a leadership position in our organization and is diligently working toward his next promotion.

A minister was intrigued by the concept of earning money through our program. The problem he faced was his fear of abusing his power from the pulpit. Once again, I found all this out in the thumbnail sketch that I conducted before I made the call. Who better to act as third-party expert than Louis Miori, a highly respected minister in Houston, Texas, and a top earner in our company? Louis, being a remarkable servant leader, gladly joined the First Look call, and the minister prospect was able to see that a peer of his has not only been successful in network marketing, but had also overcome the same fears.

Joann, a teammate from Dallas, Texas, is a very successful commercial real estate broker who has achieved the first leadership position in our company. Her realty business keeps her time at a premium. She meets many people but cannot offer the opportunity during her real estate transactions. In just the past eight days, as I write this, she gave me the thumbnail sketch info for a young high school football coach in Mansfield, Texas. We made the call while I attended a family reunion in Ohio. I mentioned that nationally famous Texas high school football coach Bob Ledbetter is our business partner. That revelation, plus the business presentation video on Joann's website, allowed me to schedule a 2-on-1 meeting in person, and the prospect even asked if he could bring others to the meeting!

Does the First Look work? You bet! The results speak for themselves. My growing business and my associates' growing businesses are the proof. I've made the First Look work for me, and now you can make it work for you.

— Ajax Daugherty

WEBINARS

A webinar uses the Internet to share your business presentation. Webinars are a great tool to use when your prospect is too busy or too far away to use another method. Your company or upline may already be using this tool. If so, then you can simply plug prospects into an already established webinar. You can also do your own private webinars; these will be more like a 1-on-1. There are plenty of great free webinar services available, and some even allow you to present right from your mobile phone or tablet computer.

The exact process and steps you take to conduct the webinar varies depending on the service provider you select. The best advice is to seek out others in your network marketing company who are using webinars successfully. They can provide advice and tips on which service they use and how to use the service most successfully.

WEBINARS

Advantages

- No boundaries. You can be in the Caribbean, with your prospect in Alaska, and you can still share your opportunity.
- Comfortable. Your prospect sees that he or she can work this business from the comfort of home.
- Time. Webinars take a lot less time because prospects have no drive time figured in to how much time they took out of their day.

Disadvantages

- Not as personal.
- Technology problems. Any time a computer is involved, you risk your prospect's having frustrations that are not related to your business at all. This is multiplied if the person you are trying to show is not tech savvy.

Guidelines

- Practice yourself before you get a guest on a webinar.
- Set a firm appointment.
- Register for your guest if a registration is required, and send him or her the login information.
- Call the prospect ten to fifteen minutes before the scheduled start time to make sure he or she has no problems getting on the webinar.
- If you are using an upline or corporate webinar, let your prospect know that you will call him or her immediately following the webinar to follow up.

HOMEWORK

We learn by doing, so let's get comfortable with your website by practicing. Practice signing in to your website. Practice sending recruiting videos to yourself and family. Get familiar with the links. Click around your website. Explore. Know what information is there and where it is. Having a great tool is of no use unless you know how to use it effectively.

Next, attend the company webinar. Yes, invite yourself. Go through the process of inviting and then attending. Yes, you. How can you lead someone else to somewhere you have not gone yourself? You can't. So get familiar by first attending yourself. Afterward, you'll feel much more capable to invite others.

Finally, once you know your website, and once you've attended, practice inviting others to the webinar and to your First Look website business presentation. This can be a great strategy to expose your friends to your business. You can now say, "John, I need to practice inviting people to my company's online webinar and to my website. Can you help me out and let me practice on you?"

You are now ready to start using First Look website presentations and webinars to recruit your team. Use the information you learned in this chapter, and get started inviting.

CHAPTER 15 – The Fortune Is in the Follow Up

When you show a business presentation, always ask the person to join your team. Once you have done that, there are really only three responses: yes, no, and maybe. If the prospect says yes, sign him or her up. That's the easy one. If your prospect says no, or your prospect says maybe, this chapter will give you some ideas on what to do.

As I have said throughout this book, success begins with how you think, with your mindset, and with your level of commitment—this applies to follow-up as well. Are you committed, or are you simply dipping your big toe in the water? A person who isn't fully committed is easily shaken by rejection, but a professional, one who is fully committed, knows that no doesn't mean no. It means not now.

THREE CHARACTER TRAITS

Some people follow up well, while others don't. I believe this skill is a result of specific character traits embedded in some people but void in others. I'd like to share three key character traits that I believe must be developed for you to master the art of follow up. All three can be learned if you try. Here are the three character traits:

1. You must be positive.
2. You must be patient.
3. You must be persistent.

BE POSITIVE

When someone doesn't answer our follow-up phone call, we immediately want to jump to conclusions. "She's not interested," is the story that plays in the imagination of a negative person. But a positive person thinks, "Something important must have come up; I'll call her back later." It's the same situation, yet two different interpretations. The stories that play in our heads will be either positive or negative. Always choose to play the positive tape in your head.

BE PATIENT

Recently, I was reading in *Men's Health* Magazine about Hollywood legend Stephen McPherson, the past President of ABC Entertainment. He's credited with shows like *Grey's Anatomy, Lost,* and *Dancing with the Stars.* A particular question came up about Mr. McPherson's passion for wine. His answer grabbed my attention. He said, "Our cabernet is in-barrel for thirty months." It was a random fact, yet it blew my mind! Before this article, I had no idea wine had to sit in a barrel for thirty months! I began to consider what kind of patience it would take to be a vintner, a maker of fine wine. How frustrating it would be that it takes thirty months—almost three years—before you can taste the results of your labor!

The reality is that all types of business demand patience. Ask any traditional business owner, and he or she will tell you that it usually takes three to five years to turn a profit. So, whether it's creating a cabernet, opening a hardware store, or building your home-based business, understand that all businesses require patience. Develop patience in your networking business, and apply that patience to your follow-up efforts.

BE PERSISTENT

Keep following up. Consider the fact that it took Noah Webster thirty-six years to write *Webster's Dictionary.* Can you imagine the persistence of this man? Persistence comes from having a mission. It comes from having a clear vision of where you're going. It comes from having a goal and a dream that is greater than any obstacle.

THE MAGIC RULE FOR FOLLOW UP

I want to share with you my rule for how to follow up effectively with prospects. When you follow this rule, you'll always have control of the process.

CHAPTER FIFTEEN: THE FORTUNE IS IN THE FOLLOW UP

When this rule becomes second nature, your business will soar. Here is the rule: Always schedule the next conversation.

Here's what I mean: Imagine your friend Sue tells you, "I'll call you after I watch the DVD." Well, according to my rule, you must schedule the next conversation. This means you must schedule a specific time to talk to Sue, or it could get awkward. You would reply to Sue, "Excellent! Call me. But if I don't hear from you, I'll call you at four o'clock Thursday."

You see, the beauty of this rule is that you remain in control. By scheduling the next conversation, you're controlling the process in a professional way. And your prospect will appreciate that.

To continue our example, let's imagine that on Thursday at four, you call Sue back. She picks up and says, "I can't talk now. Let's talk tomorrow." You would then say, "No problem. I'll call you tomorrow at 5:15." Again, you're always scheduling the next conversation.

What if Sue doesn't answer and you are forced to leave voicemail? Here's how you'd schedule the next conversation on a voice message: "Sue, sorry I missed you. Call me back. But if I don't hear from you, I'll call you tomorrow at 5:15."

Continue this chain, never letting it break. Always schedule a specific time for the next conversation. This simple rule can work magic for your business.

Setting the next conversation also works immediately after showing a presentation, when your prospect says maybe . . . and he or she can say "maybe" many different ways. He can say that he needs to talk to his spouse, pray about the decision, do some due diligence, think about it, and so on. I have the same response no matter how my prospect says maybe.

When my prospect says he needs to talk to his spouse, I say, "Great! You talk to your spouse, and I will call you tomorrow to see what you have decided."

When she says she needs to pray about her decision, I say, "Great! You pray about it, and I will call you tomorrow to see what you have decided."

When he says he wants to do some due diligence, I say, "Great! You do your due diligence, and I will call you tomorrow to see what you have decided."

You get the idea. If your prospect tells you maybe, keep scheduling the next appointment.

IF YOUR PROSPECT SAYS NO, USE THE SIX-MONTH RULE

"Would it be okay if I followed up with you in six months?" These are great words to ask anyone who rejects your opportunity, and just about every time, that person will say, "Sure, call me in six months." A name stays on my list until that person either joins my team or dies. It's that simple. I believe people give up too quickly on other people. I believe we must have a long-term mindset and understand that the timing must be just right. This brings us full circle back to our commitment. If we're committed, we don't care how long it takes. If we truly believe in our business, and if we truly care about the other person, we'll come back, and keep coming back, as long as it takes.

COACH'S SUCCESS TIP:

RECYCLE YOUR LIST EVERY SIX MONTHS.

Every six months, recycle through your contact list. I can promise you that two things will be different in six months: the timing will be different, and you will be different. You will be a different and better person six months from today. Your skills will have improved. You'll have better stories to share. Your paycheck will be bigger. And you'll have grown into a better human being because of your networking business. You will find that your own personal development will start attracting others like a magnet. So, continue to recycle through your contact list every six months. Resolve not to scratch a single name off your list until that person either joins your team or is in the grave.

Let's recap what we do if a prospect says no or maybe. If she says no, put her on the six-month callback list. If he says maybe, schedule the next conversation. When you master the subtleties of showing the plan and following up properly, it will dramatically increase your success rate.

DON'T EVER GIVE UP

You will read in the next chapter how it took me five long months of cold, hard rejection to finally sponsor my best friend Randy Hedge into my business. Was it worth it? Well, let's just say it's been worth millions of dollars for both of us! Imagine if I had quit on Randy the first time he told me no!

Imagine if I had embraced what I call a one-shot-mentality, scratching Randy's name from my prospect list after he first rejected me. Thank the Lord I didn't!

Over the years, I've seen so many new associates use this one-shot-mentality when they talk to people. I believe this mindset is a big roadblock to success. A one-shot-mentality is the mindset of an amateur. The professional understands: the fortune is in the follow up!

A close teammate of mine, Kenny Kramer, showed his best friend our business when Kenny first joined. Kenny's buddy immediately shot down the idea and tried to steal Kenny's dream of financial freedom. Did it work? No! Kenny had committed to win. The rejection from his friend merely strengthened his resolve to succeed. His commitment to his kids, to his dream, and to his business was stronger than any single rejection. And because Kenny stayed in the game and kept following up, three years later that same friend joined Kenny's team!

TIMING IS EVERYTHING

Last summer, Jimmy exposed his brother Ryan to our business opportunity. Ryan saw the potential in the business but had no interest in joining the team. "I'm not interested," was his response. At first dejected and discouraged that his own brother had told him no, Jimmy began to consider the timing in Ryan's life . . .

You see, just two weeks prior to this, Ryan had received a promotion at the bank where he worked. He had gone from a manager to a vice president. Ryan was content, satisfied, and even happy with his job and his situation at the time he was exposed to network marketing.

However, fast-forward the calendar six months. Ryan had now discovered that the promotion at his job meant more travel, longer hours, more responsibility, Saturday work . . . and all of that for just a little extra pay. His dream job seemed more like a nightmare. Now he found himself discontent, dissatisfied, and unhappy. Because of this, when Jimmy followed up with his brother in six months, Ryan's response was, "Tell me more about that home-based business." So what had changed? The opportunity was the same. The product was the same. The presentation was the same. But the timing in Ryan's life was not the same.

"Put on a new pair of shoes."

– John C. Maxwell

Try to stand in another's shoes; see things from his or her point of view. When we do, rejection becomes less of a personal thing and more of a timing thing. We will truly understand that no really means not now. We will learn to keep following up until the timing is right.

HOMEWORK:

1. Create a reliable system to automate and organize your follow-up efforts. The system can be digitized, such as in Google Calendar, or it can be handwritten in a yearly planner. Typically, the most effective systems are those that are the most simple.

2. You might ask the most organized person you know for his or her advice.

3. Tweet your intention to get organized (include #CoachPresley)! Tell your Facebook followers that your new goal is to find a system that works for you . . . and to follow that system!

Remember: To follow up effectively, you must be organized. As soon as you schedule a follow up, write it down, get it in your system. As with any other skill, this is all learnable. It starts when you decide that you'll be organized, that you'll act as a professional in your follow-up efforts, and that you'll create a system to keep you on track.

CHAPTER 16 – How to Overcome Rejection

"I take rejection as someone blowing a bugle in my ear to wake me up and get going, rather than a retreat."

—SYLVESTER STALLONE

Whether making a contact, setting an appointment, showing a business plan, or following up, one of the biggest potential obstacles in networking is rejection. Rejection is one of the toughest human emotions that you can experience, and dealing with it is an ongoing challenge.

This isn't a new problem. From the beginning of time, people have been rejected. There was a time when everyone believed the sun revolved around the earth. A few visionaries refused to accept what everyone else believed. Their views were rejected. They risked their reputations, but Copernicus and Galileo would not give in until the rest of the world caught on: the earth revolves around the sun.

It does not matter who you are, what your background is, or how much success you achieved before you started your networking business—some people are going to tell you no.

JEANIE'S BEST FRIEND

When my company began national expansion, I was excited about the opportunity to build my business in a new area. The announcement was made, and I was thrilled because we were expanding into a state where Jeanie's best friend lived. As soon as the market opened, we called Mike and Laurie and told them we were going to be in the area and wanted to come by, catch up, and share something with them. These were friends of ours, and we were excited to share our life-changing opportunity with them. At this point, we had earned several million dollars, we were the number one money earners, and we had a monthly residual income greater than most people's annual salary. Sitting at Mike and Laurie's house, I went through our presentation as I had done a thousand times before. I even had a little more zest than usual, as Mike was a sharp businessperson. I just knew that with the company track record and our success, Mike would see it right away. When I finished, I looked up at Mike and Laurie and said, "Well, you guys are the only people we know in Georgia, and I will work with you to help you be successful. We have a chance to make a lot of money together. Let's get started."

Mike and Laurie looked at each other and said, "We are really happy for you guys, but we don't think now is the right time for us to start something new."

There it was. No. They had seen 100 percent of the information. They knew that we had great success in our home state. They even understood that they could start on the ground floor in Georgia. However, they still said no. I was disappointed, but I didn't let this slow me down. I realize that it doesn't matter how successful, brilliant, and articulate you may be, if the time is not right in the prospect's life, he or she will not join.

SARABETH ALMOST QUITS

At one point, rejection almost drove our daughter SaraBeth out of networking. But because she stayed the course, she is now one of the top young networkers in the country. As she explains, "I became a student at Baylor University shortly after getting involved in networking. Starting a networking business was a total change and forced me way out of my comfort zone. As I talked to friends, family, and fellow students about joining my team, I saw some personalities change. Some of my friends laughed, and others became distant. It bothered me when they appeared to feel that I was trying to take advantage of our friendship. Many times, I just wanted to quit and get back in my comfort zone. I really struggled with rejection for the first year in networking. But one day it hit me. Some associates on my team were thanking me for getting them involved. They started telling me how networking had changed their lives. It dawned on me that if I had quit, I would never have met all of these new friends who are so positive, motivated, and full of life."

DON'T TAKE IT PERSONALLY

Don't take rejection personally. A no or not interested response to your business is not a personal rejection of you. Think about it. If you tried to recruit your mom into your business, and she was content with her life and told you not interested, would you consider it personal rejection? Of course not! It's not about you; it's about the business. People aren't rejecting you: it's just not the right time in their lives. Top money earners learn early in their career to ignore rejection and move on to the next prospect. Some will, some won't, so what—who's next?

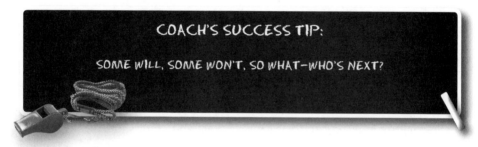

COACH'S SUCCESS TIP:

SOME WILL, SOME WON'T, SO WHAT—WHO'S NEXT?

THE RANDY HEDGE STORY

If someone says no to your opportunity, she is saying no . . . at this time. Things change in people's lives, and if you treat the prospect with respect and leave her with a positive experience, there is a good chance a time will come when she will join your team.

Reflect with me on my discussions with my best friend. I think it really illustrates how sometimes we need to let it go and keep our sights on another day when the time is right.

When I got involved with my current company, I couldn't wait to talk to my best friend Randy Hedge. One of our favorite pastimes is hunting. It was deer season, and I couldn't get to Arkansas fast enough. We were going to have some fun, and I was going to share my new opportunity with Randy. The first evening of camp, we were sitting around the campfire, and I had my hunting bucket close by. I whipped out my pad and showed Randy the business. He said, "No, Presley, it's just not for me, buddy."

I knew that he had a lot going on in his life at that point, so I replied, "Sure, no problem. I'll keep you posted on how I'm doing." That was all that was said about the business at that time.

A month or two went by, and Randy and I were together again. He asked, "How's the new business going?" We talked about it for a couple of minutes, and it was dropped again. Another month or two passed, and we discussed it again. After about five months, Randy said, "Hey, Presley, I'd like to take a look at that business again." I shared the opportunity with him and, at that point, he said, "I'm in, buddy."

As they say, the rest is history. He's the number six money earner in our company. It's been life changing for Randy, and he's been a huge part of my team.

The point of the story is that if someone tells you no, it simply may not be a good time in his life. But remember, life has a way of changing. Someone who is not interested today can very well be interested tomorrow.

NEGATIVE PEOPLE

When someone says no to our business, most of the time it is the timing in a prospect's life, but sometimes it's just the person. Some people in our world are just negative. Period. It doesn't matter what you do or show them, they are not going to do anything to change their lives. They would rather be miserable because it gives them something to complain about. If they were happy, they wouldn't have anything to complain about, and that would make them miserable. When they reject you, it is about them, not you. When you run across a negative person, say "next" and move on to the next person on your list. When these naysayers arise, remember to consider the source. I always say, "Never listen to or take advice from people more screwed up than you are!"

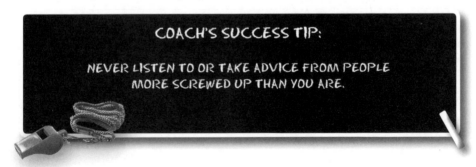

COACH'S SUCCESS TIP:

NEVER LISTEN TO OR TAKE ADVICE FROM PEOPLE MORE SCREWED UP THAN YOU ARE.

"DID SOMEONE MENTION A BARN?"

I have been networking for a long time, but I still get surprised occasionally. Get a load of this story—once again involving Randy Hedge.

Randy called me and said, "I'm going to show a presentation, and I want you to go with me." I thought to myself, "My gosh, you've made millions of dollars in networking. You don't need me."

But Randy went on to explain that the guy used to be a basketball official and he owns a sporting goods store. "I think y'all might have a lot in common. You probably know a lot of the same people. Would you come and talk to this guy with me?"

Obviously, I said, "Sure, I'm happy to."

We met at a restaurant called Poor Richards in Richardson, Texas. The prospect came in, we visited a while, and we did have a lot in common. We reminisced about the past and who had done what.

After a good visit, I got my presentation book out and showed Randy's prospect a presentation. Anybody who has watched me show a presentation knows that I'm passionate about what I do. I went through the presentation in about fifteen minutes, closed my book, looked at the guy, and said, "Listen, we've got a chance to make a lot of money. Let's get you started. Let's get you on the team."

I can remember vividly to this day. After hearing the presentation, the guy sat back in his chair, and the first words out of his mouth were, "The zoning commission won't let me build a barn behind my house."

These were literally the first words out of his mouth. In our conversations, before and during the presentation, we hadn't talked about a barn or his house or the zoning commission. Then out of the clear blue, this guy blurts out, "The zoning commission won't let me build a barn behind my house."

I packed my stuff up, looked at Randy, and said, "Listen buddy, I'm going to let you finish this one." I shook the guy's hand and left.

Here's the point . . . it doesn't matter who's presenting. You can't say the right thing to the wrong one or the wrong thing to the right one. You had the number-one money earner and the number-six money earner presenting, and the guy didn't get in. I'm not even sure he was listening! If the time is right in prospects' lives, they get in; if it's not, they don't.

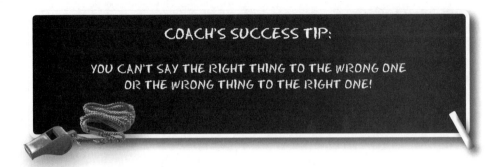

COACH'S SUCCESS TIP:

YOU CAN'T SAY THE RIGHT THING TO THE WRONG ONE OR THE WRONG THING TO THE RIGHT ONE!

A TIP TO HELP MINIMIZE REJECTION

Posture

Posture is probably the most underestimated skill a networker can learn. Posture refers to your attitude when you are talking to others about your business, when you are setting an appointment, when you are showing the plan, or when you are following up. Posture—or how you carry and present yourself when conducting or discussing your network marketing business—can directly affect the amount of rejection you experience. Always sound confident and strong about what you are doing. This creates attraction and limits objections and rejections from others who may want to join you.

People often say, "It's easy for you to talk strong, Presley. You have already made millions of dollars." The secret is that I was talking in a purposeful, confident, and deliberate manner long before I made my first dollar. If you want to have the right posture, you must have an all-in mentality.

Imagine Winston Churchill telling his troops, "I think we might defeat the Nazis; we will try it for a little while and see how it goes." Do you think people would follow a leader like that? Stop being a big-toe-in-the-water networker—dive in head first! I promise the water is great in the pool. Believe in the profession, believe in your company, and, most importantly, believe in yourself.

Here are some practical things that will improve your posture:

1. Make eye contact.
2. Smile big.
3. Speak up.
4. Walk fast.
5. Have high energy.
6. Always have a winning attitude.

The Takeaway

When talking to prospects, confidence should exude from your voice. When you are confident, prospects will sense your power and be drawn to it. In face-to-face meetings, if a prospect has an attitude and keeps raising objections, simply pick up your material, thank him for his time, shake his hand, and start walking. This will empower you, and—believe it or not—a lot of the time, prospects will ask you to come back. The fear of loss is powerful. When you present your opportunity and then withdraw it, it tends to create a fear of loss. Your unwillingness to argue will give you a huge psychological advantage.

I also believe that if your prospects realize that you don't really care if they say yes or no, they will let down their guard, and you will have a much more productive meeting. In fact, if we spend too much time debating or trying to convince someone, our efforts may be detrimental to our future success with that prospect. Ask yourself, "Do I want to be right, or do I want to be rich?"

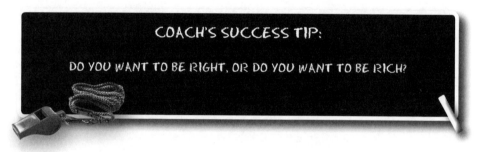

COACH'S SUCCESS TIP:

DO YOU WANT TO BE RIGHT, OR DO YOU WANT TO BE RICH?

"The world has the habit of making room for the man whose words and actions show that he knows where he is going."

— NAPOLEON HILL

IT'S UP TO YOU!

If you have a dream, you will know where you are going, and so will those around you. You will send out a message to people that you are going somewhere in life. Your message will say, "I am on the road to success and, if you join my team, you can be successful, too!"

People want to be part of a winning team. When you are determined to reach your dreams, you will tap into an inner power that you may not have realized you possess. This inner power will help you overcome the rejections, objections, challenges, and fears that get in the way.

I've seen some of the most gifted people in the world accomplish little with their lives. Not because they lack ambition, not because they don't have a dream, and not because they are afraid of work. They have accomplished little simply because fear of rejection and the unknown had a hold on them that wouldn't let go. Remember, courage is not the absence of fear, but the realization that something in our life is more important than fear. The only person who can hold you back is you. Remember these words, "If it's to be, it's up to me." You can have a life of financial and time freedom or a life of mediocrity . . . it is all up to you!

HOMEWORK

Consider rereading the previous section, "It's Up to You." Notice that a trend in the book that I keep going back to is this idea of having a dream, a vision, and a goal. Someone once said, "Grab ahold of your vision until it grabs ahold of you." Once our vision grabs us, we'll have no issue handling rejection. Rejection will then become merely a bug on the windshield on our road to success!

The following is how you can grab a hold of your vision long enough until it grabs a hold of you:

1. First, write your goals down every morning as soon as you wake. This focuses your thoughts for the day.

2. Next, rewrite your goals just before going to bed. This employs your mind to be thinking of ways to accomplish your goals, even while you sleep.

3. And last, any time you feel down, you're hit by rejection, or things didn't turn out just the way you wanted—at that moment, rewrite your goals once more!

4. Tweet about a rejection you once encountered. Let your followers know they're not alone. We all face rejection.

5. Post one of your goals to your Facebook wall (and my Facebook wall www.facebook.com/presleyswagerty); sharing helps us hold ourselves accountable.

This is so important. By writing down your goals, you're refocusing your mind on the positive, on what it is that's driving you. You're refocusing on your destination. When your mind is that focused, no bug on the windshield (rejection) will detour you from reaching your dream!

CHAPTER 17 – Obtain Huge Results Quickly

MASSIVE AND IMMEDIATE ACTION

Do you like to get out of the gate quickly? Do you want to build a full-time income in a short time? Are you someone who wants to see major results quickly?

If so, you will want to start your business with a 30-Day Press. Back in my coaching days, I picked up the pace in our basketball games with a full-court press. This is a basketball strategy that refers to a defensive style in which the defense applies either man-to-man or zone pressure the entire length of the court. A full-court press takes a great deal of effort, but can be very effective at picking up the speed of the game.

A 30-Day Press is like the full-court press of your network marketing business. Essentially, it means you will show business presentations to large numbers of people in a short time. For serious business builders, we can condense a year's worth of work into a month, a month's worth of work into a week, and a week's worth of work into a day. The 30-Day Press is only for those willing to push the envelope and take massive and immediate action.

THE GOAL

The goal of the 30-Day Press is to complete a minimum of thirty live business presentations for you and/or for your team in the first thirty days in the business. This will require you to get your top prospects in front of the presentation immediately. You will then do the same for all your new associates. The more prospects you have in your pipeline, the more new associates you will help begin their businesses.

A SIMPLE PLAN

Bruce Lee, the famous martial artist, said, "I fear not the man who has practiced 10,000 kicks once; but I fear the man who has practiced one kick 10,000 times." You see, Bruce Lee understood the value of simplicity, of mastering the basics through repetition.

It is easy to overcomplicate the process when massive action is about to be taken. Resist that temptation. This is a simple business. I have always found that simplicity works best. Simplicity gives you the ability to duplicate, and duplication will create leverage. Only through leverage can you achieve the momentum that can result in rapid, exponential growth.

I endorse a simple, three-step system. If you focus all your energy on these three simple actions, you will be amazed at what is possible. Jeanie and I have been blessed to earn almost $20 million by staying focused on these three simple tasks and teaching others to do the same.

COACH'S SUCCESS TIP:

PLUG IN TO MEETINGS.
SET APPOINTMENTS.
SHOW THE PLAN.

That's it! People come up to me all the time, pull me aside, and say, "Come on, Presley, you can tell me. What's your secret?" I reply, "Plug into meetings, set appointments, and show the plan."

Then they'll say, "No, no Presley. Seriously, what's the real secret?" And I say, "Plug into meetings, set appointments, and show the plan."

They look at me puzzled and say, "You don't understand, Presley! I want to make millions like you!" Then I say, "Well, you've really got to plug into LOTS of meetings, set LOTS of appointments, and show LOTS of plans."

It's not a joke, guys. The truth is . . . simple works best.

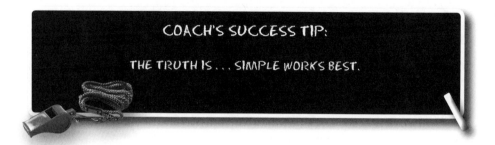

COACH'S SUCCESS TIP:

THE TRUTH IS . . . SIMPLE WORKS BEST.

TAKE ACTION

The best way to see results in your 30-Day Press is to get on the phone and start setting appointments. Appointment setting is a necessary daily activity for the serious builder. You hear top networkers from across the world say, "Master the invitation, and you'll master the business." There is simply no substitute for working the phone. You must set appointments and show the plan daily to build momentum in your first thirty days.

USE A VARIETY OF PRESENTATION METHODS

1-on-1s, 2-on-1s, hotel events, webinars, and website videos are all great, but a way to explode your 30-Day Press is to host home meetings. Schedule two or three home meetings at your home or the home of your sponsor the very first week you begin the 30-Day Press. Then repeat this process by helping your new associates do multiple home meetings their first week as well.

The only way to have a successful 30-Day Press is for you to get in the trenches and lead by example. Remember, this is a monkey see, monkey do business. Be the leader you aspire to find.

MOMENTUM

Momentum is a precious commodity in networking. This is a great time to discuss momentum because a 30-Day Press can often create it. Momentum is a strange thing to try to explain. Momentum is the biggest factor in average becoming extraordinary.

Before I got into networking, I had experienced momentum on the basketball court. This is where I learned valuable lessons about how powerful a force momentum can be. During that same period, I also learned that it is much easier to keep momentum than to try to get it back. As a coach, I could always feel which team was gaining momentum. It is a strange force on the basketball court when your opponent has momentum. It can feel like you're playing against a team with an extra man on the court. When my team got momentum, I pushed them even harder. I knew this was the time to take advantage of what we had. When I began networking, I carried this lesson into my new business. When I felt a group gaining momentum, I pushed harder, I made more calls, and I did more presentations.

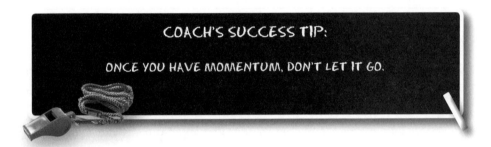

COACH'S SUCCESS TIP:

ONCE YOU HAVE MOMENTUM, DON'T LET IT GO.

Now that statement may sound obvious, but obvious or not, it has a huge impact. Momentum is such a factor in building a big organization, and I want you to take that tip to heart. Momentum is not something you want to take for granted once you have it. Once you get momentum, it's a great time to execute another 30-Day Press to send it into overdrive. In the unfortunate circumstance that you lose momentum, a 30-Day Press is your best hope for regaining it.

REPEAT THE PROCESS FREQUENTLY

While it is impossible to maintain this type of pace for long periods, it is important to repeat the 30-Day Press frequently. It is imperative to teach the 30-Day Press to your new team members, whether you personally sponsor them or they come into your group in depth.

Understand that, even if you teach it to your entire team, only some will answer the challenge and show you they are true business builders. This is a great indicator that someone has decided to change his life and stand in the gap for his family. It shows you she is willing to work hard and be coachable. An individual who jumps at the opportunity to do a 30-Day Press right out of the gate is showing you that he or she has a burning desire to succeed. Pour yourself into these pacesetters, and help them build their teams and develop their leadership skills. After all, their successes are also your successes.

Once again, there is no substitute for a real example. When my company began its national expansion, it was much anticipated. The effort had been months in the making and I, along with other top earners in the field, had been building excitement among our ranks.

One of the leaders I respect most is a guy who has given his all to the organization as a whole. Not only is he a true field leader, he has also made a total personal commitment to the crusade by volunteering to lead all of our major company training events. He really is a pro. Anyone who has seen him in action will admit there is no close second. His name is Brian Lucia.

National expansion was a much-anticipated change in our team's way of life. It was not just an event. That said, when the announcement came to get started, we were ready to go; we took massive and immediate action. The 30-Day Press was underway! Here's how Brian remembers it:

National expansion was everything we had been building and preparing for over the previous five years. Presley, I, and the other leaders in the company had been feverishly pushing ourselves to the limit while coaching our teams to give their all as well. We wanted those who were up to the challenge to be on top of their games when the expansion launched. And we were.

We prepared by rehearsing our game plan time after time on team conference calls. But more than that, we repetitively practiced the 30-Day Press right in our own backyards. We didn't know when expansion would occur exactly, but we knew it would be soon, and we wanted to be ready. You see, luck is simply Labor Under Correct Knowledge, and to have luck, you must put yourself in a position of opportunity.

Preparation is key, but there are other ingredients. Some we control more than others. One thing we can control is focusing our prospecting efforts on successful people.

When the company fired the starting pistol for expansion, I reached out to my team. I said, "Okay, guys, this is our chance. Get me in front of the most successful people you know in the new market."

When my friend and teammate Richard Desmond introduced me to Chip Lever, I didn't know he was going to be a superstar, but I knew he was a person of success and influence, and that was all I needed to know at that time. I simply said to Chip on the phone after we had a brief get-to-know-you chat, "Look, I'm going to fly up there in two days. Can you put five or ten of the most successful people you know in a room to hear what I have to say?"

Chip, a successful person, had heard all he needed to hear. He said yes and joined as an associate immediately. That was on a Monday. That Wednesday, I walked into the meeting with Chip, and he delivered. There sat six of the most successful people in the area.

I shared about the company, the opportunity, and the breadth of what we had our hands on. They were all listening intently and could sense from my urgency, enthusiasm, and conviction that time was of the essence. Then I laid out the plan for the 30-Day-Press. I could see that these guys not only understood, but they would also deliver. I made the same call to action I had made to Chip: "I need each of you to have five to ten people here with you next Wednesday." And just like that, it was over. There were no excuses and no quibbling. These were men of action.

At the next meeting, there were fifty-two people in the room. We went from one person to six, then to fifty-two in just sixteen short days. The new associates followed the lead of the six leaders who set it all in motion, and in just a few months, the team numbered in the thousands. All of this resulted from everyone's bringing three to five people each week.

There were two additional keys to the success of the group as a whole. One, the leaders stayed engaged by phone with the new associates and emerging leaders throughout each week, not just on meeting Wednesdays. We'd say things like, "Who couldn't make the meeting last night we could go see?" or, "Who can we help you follow up with?" or, "Great job last night! I got to meet your three guests," or, "Let's not wait until next Wednesday. Who can I help you share the information with today?" We maintained the urgency and enthusiasm constantly and instilled that in the entire team. Second, we put an emphasis on "the meeting before the meeting" and "the meeting after the meeting." Whether it was business building and training tips, question answering, or just getting to know each other better, we created a culture of "get there early and stay late." Everyone couldn't wait for the meeting on Wednesdays, and the excitement filtered through to the prospects also.

Does it always happen like this? No. The point is this: when the perfect storm comes, you must be ready. Practice the skills every day, even when it takes an extra effort. When bad times come, you aren't as bad as you think. You are a product of your preparation and mindset.

The key is not to be caught off guard. Be positioned. Do the right things every day. Stay focused, stay positive, stay engaged, and when the opportunity hits, do a 30-Day Press and watch your team explode.

—Brian Lucia

HOMEWORK

What time is it? It's time to take action. Now is the time to start your 30-Day Press:

1. First, decide on a start date. Nothing happens until you begin. Tweet or post to Facebook your intention to start a 30-Day Press. Include #CoachPresley and post them to my Facebook wall www.facebook.com/presleyswagerty, too. When others ask you what that means, here's your chance to invite them!

2. Next, decide your activity goal: how many people will you expose your business to in the next thirty days for yourself and for your team? The minimum is thirty, but you decide your own activity goal. If your goal is sixty, you then know you must average two a day for thirty days. How many you decide upon isn't as important as deciding on a number and committing to reaching it.

3. I'm a visual person, and maybe you are too. So let's set up a visual aid for your 30-Day Press. Consider using a piece of poster board and mapping out a 30-day calendar. At the top, write "30-Day Press." Highlight your start date and your end date for your 30-Day Press. You'll put this calendar on your bathroom mirror or any place where you see it often. This is a visual reminder of your 30-day mission.

4. Then start showing the business at the pace you've set for yourself. Every time you show the business, mark your poster-board calendar accordingly. Nothing is more motivating than progress. As you see your poster board fill up, a result of your showing the business, the visual progress will excite you, and you'll find it easier and easier to keep moving forward!

One last thought. Do NOT focus on results during this 30-Day Press. Focus on activity: showing the business X number of times in thirty days. Results tend to lag behind. Put your head down and simply complete your 30-Day Press activity regardless of the results. The truth about results is this: by the time you see results, the work will have been done long before!

CHAPTER 18 – Team Building 101

"Talent wins games, but teamwork and intelligence wins championships."

— MICHAEL JORDAN

If you want to create wealth in networking, you must realize it is not just about what you do. Massive success in networking is the result of team building. All network marketing opportunities are about building a massive team in which each member gathers a handful of customers. It continues to amaze me how many people fail to grasp this concept. It is the "network" in network marketing that creates the wealth machine. Consider this example.

As I write this, I average about one hundred new associates per day joining my network marketing team. Let's just use an example of two customers per associate for easy math. Assuming each of these one hundred associates gathers just two customers—that's 200 customers added to my organization every day! How many of us could go out individually and gather 200 customers today, much less day after day after day?

ATTRACTION BUSINESS

If you have a dream, you will know where you are going, and so will everyone around you. You will send out a message to the people you talk to that you are going somewhere in life. Your message will be, "I am on the road to success and, if you join my team, you can be successful, too!"

We are in the attraction business, and we must make our business exciting to attract people to our team. I always say, "If you are fired up, people will come from miles around to watch you burn." We must think big because those who think big attract successful people. We must put the fun back in fundamentals. Additionally, we must create a sense of urgency: create an atmosphere that we are going to do something great—NOW!

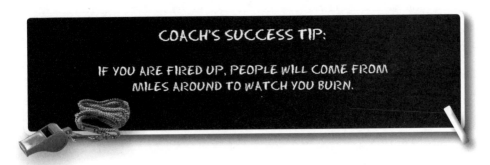

COACH'S SUCCESS TIP:

IF YOU ARE FIRED UP, PEOPLE WILL COME FROM MILES AROUND TO WATCH YOU BURN.

People want to feel as though they are a part of something bigger than themselves. We must create an environment in which associates grow, become connected, and feel like they are part of a team that is going somewhere. It's all about the culture. You must take control and create a positive culture for your team.

> *"Ask not what your teammates can do for you. Ask what you can do for your teammates."*
>
> **—MAGIC JOHNSON**

TEAM CULTURE

Culture is the spiritual fabric between us that champions the crusade. It supports belief in the organization and holds us together as a team. The cultural fabric is servant leadership, personal growth, integrity, work ethic, and following the simple system. Our culture is what makes us winners and ensures we rise to the top. It helps us achieve greatness and lead the crusade against debt and financial worries. In short, culture is who we are (our values), where we are going (the crusade), and how we will get there (the system).

You meet special people on your networking journey, and the young man whose story you are about to enjoy is, without a doubt, one of the most special people I know. David Adams has accomplished a ton in his time on this Earth, but where he's headed will make his accomplishments to date pale in comparison. A very big part of that success comes from the lessons he learned from the experience he shares with us here.

TINA TURNER, TREY DYER, AND THE DAY MY BUSINESS CHANGED

I can remember the day my network marketing business changed forever. There I was, sitting second row. The room was packed, as business associates squeezed into chairs and lined the walls to hear the great Trey Dyer speak from the stage.

Trey had just broken into the prestigious Top 10 Money Earners list inside our billion-dollar company. Out of 250,000-plus entrepreneurs, Trey was in the Top 10! But how? He was from a small town. So was I. He had joined our company late; so did I. He had never done networking before; neither had I. So how did Trey break into the elite Top 10? What was his secret?

As Trey took the stage, the loudspeakers blasted Tina Turner's "Simply the Best" hit single. For a few moments, our crowd of normal, everyday business professionals morphed into thirteen-year-old schoolgirls clamoring for Justin Bieber! Chills came over me. Trey had hit rock star status in our company, and I was determined to hear exactly how.

Trey's small 5'10" frame beamed with confidence as he reached the microphone. He had a contagious smile, sort of a child-like grin that communicated, "I've got something special." His smile captivated the crowd. We hushed. And Trey, with a warm southern Texas drawl, began sharing his story.

To this day, I forget most of what he said. In fact, I only remember one sentence from his thirty-minute monologue. But one was plenty. One blurb effectively turned my business completely in a new direction. So let me share Trey Dyer's statement with you.

"The difference between a team of 100 and a team of 10,000 is culture."

Culture Defined

I had heard the word before: culture. But what did that mean in the circle of networking? Was this new insight?

Later that night, I went to the Internet to get a firm definition of culture. I found this: "Culture is the attitudes and behavior characteristics of a particular social group."

In essence, Trey had purposefully instilled behaviors and attitudes into his team that he was crediting for his success. What were they? What attitudes? What behaviors? Looking for an answer had only led me to more questions.

On Purpose or by Default

As I rode home on the plane after the event, Trey's quote had my head spinning. By its definition, I realized my team already had a culture. My team already had an attitude. By default, we already were acting a certain way.

For example, my team didn't value big events. My communication to my teammates in the past was something like, "Come when or if you can." Events were just not that important. Another example is how we treated the idea of personal growth. Yes, I was undergoing a personal transformation by listening to audio programs and reading good books. However, at the time, I thought that was just for me . . . I didn't need to bother my teammates with it. That's how I felt.

So at the top of my journal page, I wrote, "My Team's CURRENT Culture." The laundry list included everything you don't want a team to be. Evidently, by not being purposeful about the attitudes and behaviors we stood for as a team, a laundry list of apathetic qualities had taken root by default. I was reminded of Jim Rohn's quote: "If you rest too long, the weeds take the garden." How true. On that plane ride, I realized that every team, my team included, already has a culture. And like a garden, if we haven't planted and fertilized what we want, then what we don't want takes over . . . like weeds.

On that plane ride, I committed to developing a strong team culture of attitudes and behaviors that would lead to better results. It just made sense that, if there was going to be a culture anyway, it might as well be one that leads to duplication and wealth.

At that time, I began a journey to develop such a culture. I became a student of the dozens of leaders who were more successful than I was. What exactly did they do? What attitudes did they encourage? What actions? What behaviors?

I would begin by learning more about Trey Dyer.

Very quickly, I noticed something profound: Trey Dyer was no genius. Trey Dyer simply modeled after other successful people. He, like I did, studied the cultural aspects of other successful leaders in our profession. Trey started as a master student and then became a master duplicator of attitudes and behaviors that generated the best results. So why recreate the wheel? If he could do it, so could I. And so can you.

The Shopping Cart

When we look at the vast possibilities of attitudes, qualities, actions, and behaviors that we can use to build a strong team culture, the possibilities are endless. I relate this to shopping at a grocery store. With 10,000 different items to select from, each leader is going to select items for his or her shopping cart in accordance with individual personality and philosophy. Every shopper is different; every leader is different. What I put in my buggy isn't necessarily what's right for you and your situation. And the reverse is true . . . and that's okay.

Let me share with you eight things you'll find in my cart. I've successfully built a strong culture by focusing on these eight. Allow yourself to decide whether these eight are right for you and your situation. You might not be keen on a few, and there might be one or two things on your grocery list that you won't find on mine. That's fine. But again, the results I've created from focusing on these eight are significant. Let's take a look . . .

EIGHT ELEMENTS OF A STRONG TEAM CULTURE

1. Having High Energy

Decide today that you're going to be a person of high energy. This is a decision. All it takes is a moment. One moment. Decide now that you're a person of strong, positive, and high energy. The sooner you make this decision for yourself, the sooner your business will explode.

What exactly do I mean? Well, before I made this decision for myself, a typical phone call from a teammate might go something like this . . .

"Dave, hey, it's Larry. How are you?"

"Uh [yawn], Larry, you have no idea how tired I am. Yesterday a lady kept yappin' about who-knows-what . . . the appointment was supposed to take just thirty minutes . . . but it went on for two hours! I'm whupped. What can I do for you?"

How pathetic. How sad. I want to go back and slap that old version of myself and say, "Wake up, David! Get some energy!"

Fortunately, I changed. I decided to be somebody who showed up with energy and passion. So now, no matter which teammate calls, I pick the phone up with energy. There are no exceptions. For example, the other day when I was in a bookstore, my phone rang. I realized that if I were to answer, I would have to whisper. No way I was going to whisper so I fast paced outside the double doors and then, with a booming-confident-positive voice, I answered, "Maria! Hey! It's great to hear from you! How was your weekend?"

Art Williams is famous for saying, "Winners stay excited for as long as it takes." It's time we all make a decision to get excited, stay excited, and come with energy! No exceptions. Presley has always taught, "If you want your team to be excited, then you get excited." I can't say it any better than that. Let's get excited! Let's come with energy! Let's purposefully instill a culture of excited and energetic teammates. If you do that, your business will attract others as energetic as you are.

2. Having Fun

It's been said, "People who play together stay together." In my business, I've found this to be true.

My brother Sean is great at pool. When we compete, just when I think he doesn't have a shot, Sean will aim the white cue ball away from his target, toward a vacant side of the table, and execute a brilliant bank shot to hammer in his targeted ball. How does this relate? Well, in my case, and likely yours, money is the target. We're after results. We're after new teammates and new customers. I would argue that if we aim at that, we likely won't hit our target. However, when we turn our aim toward people having fun, we execute a bank shot and reach our target.

Look at your company. It's likely the top leaders in your firm are some of the most fun people to be around. They're always smiling and laughing. By simply being around them, happiness is contagious. The danger here is to assume, "Well, they can smile now because they're making all that money. They don't know what it's really like to struggle." I would venture to say that they've always been smiling. They've always been having a good time. Sure, they've had hard times, but they've always made the most of it. Before they got their first check, I imagine they smiled when their brother-in-law told them no. Whether we have a team of two, twenty, or 20,000, let's create a culture of people having fun. How do we do that? There are several ways. Allow me to share a few.

First, make sure that you're having fun. Make sure you love what you do. If you're having fun, then your teammates will pick up on that.

Second, don't take yourself too seriously. Not taking yourself too seriously is a sign of good self-esteem and confidence. A leader with high self-confidence has the ability to laugh at his or her own mistakes. Good leaders tell stories about their screw-ups and laugh at past blunders. They relate stories of their own misfortunes to humor their teammates, and also to encourage them.

Third, coordinate team parties. I encourage a monthly party for your team in each area in which your business has fifteen or more associates. These parties should be fun. They are not times for training or correction. A party is a party. If there is training involved, then the training should be fun and humorous. Get your teammates spending time laughing with one another, bonding, and creating relationships through a shared, positive experience such as a team party.

The fourth way to help create this culture is to collect stories. Be a collector of fun stories shared by others. Tell these stories. It's fun to hear a fun story about the "struggle turned triumph" of someone else in our profession. Any story that causes a good laugh is a way to lighten up presentations and formal business overviews.

Celebrating successes is the fifth way to instill a fun culture. We'll talk about this later . . . this idea of celebrating achievements.

The sixth way is to get paid. Money is fun! Let's admit that up front. Help your teammates get paid. Create a culture of teammates getting checks. We'll talk more about this later as well.

Seventh, I suggest having a "meeting after the meeting." Gather up the troops and head over to a restaurant for a sandwich once the formal stuff is over. Or migrate from the business meeting to a local ice cream parlor or coffee shop. It's important to make time after the formal meeting to create personal connections with teammates. If your group is massive, then focus on spending this time with the producers . . . those who deserve your time and attention. During this time, I recommend discussing things not related to your business. Have fun. Talk sports. Tell jokes. Get to know your teammates.

3. Learning and Growing
Jim Rohn, the father of personal development, said, "Formal education will make you a living. But self-education will make you a fortune."

When I was younger, I hated olives. Disgusting! Black olives, green olives, any olive . . . it didn't matter. They were gross. The smell made me sick. How can people eat them? That's how I felt about olives. Funny thing was I had never tried an olive before. But here I was in my twenties . . . I hated olives, and I didn't know why. Then one day, I tried an olive. Turns out, I not only liked olives, I loved them! Black olives, green olives . . . all olives! I love them all. If I eat one, I'll eat the whole jar. I just needed a taste.

I relate my hatred for olives to my contempt for personal development. Before I tasted personal development, I would see people like Anthony Robbins and, as an outsider looking in, say, "Who is that cheese ball?" I hated the idea of voluntary learning. "Why read?" I would ask. "I am done with school. I got my diploma." I was completely shut off to the idea of self-education. But I had never tried it. I had never tasted it. Then I stumbled onto a Jim Rohn audio program, and I was hooked. Today, I love personal development. I can't get enough. Like with olives, I just needed a taste.

Darren Hardy, in an interview with Eric Worre on NetworkMarketingPro.com, says, "People join network marketing companies for the money and for the opportunity. But they stay because of the relationships and the personal growth." Out of everything I've ever heard or read I find this quote to be one of the most useful phrases in building a strong team. Once a teammate joins, as leaders, it's imperative that we bring him or her into a culture of personal growth. Personal growth is not just something to encourage . . . it's what we do. We read books. We listen to audio. We turn our car into a university on wheels. And we do this because we know personal growth is the glue that can keep a teammate from quitting.

Presley has always said, "This is a monkey see, monkey do business." We start a team culture of personal growth and self-development by growing ourselves. Jim Rohn talks about one of the most powerful words being the word "Let's!" As in, "Let's go do it." Not, "You go do it." Rather than tell our teammates, "You go read this book," we'll get better results when we approach teammates, saying, "Let's go read this book." This is how we start a team culture of personal growth.

Let me share a few final thoughts on personal growth. The book you don't read won't help; this is another concept from Jim Rohn that revolutionized my perception on reading and growing. I'm glad to share that with you. How true. Presley taught me early on that not being a good reader is no excuse. "That's why they make books on CDs . . . for people like us who don't like to read."

Literally, we have no excuses. Get yourself and your teammates on a path of personal development. Once you taste progress, you'll be hooked!

4. Recognizing

In Randy Gage's book *How to Build a Multi-Level Money Machine*, he talks about the army in a powerful comparison to our networking profession. He says that what really motivates soldiers to endure through hardships and enemy fire is the recognition of fellow soldiers.

People, no matter what they tell you, crave praise. They don't want praise. They don't desire praise. They crave it. Crave is the best word to describe what we feel in regard to recognition. I know because I'm no different. I want the stage. I crave the praise. I want my fellow soldiers to give me recognition! And I'd venture to say you are no different.

But here's something interesting. I've learned to satisfy my personal craving by dishing out recognition and praise to my teammates. Try it. This is a fascinating truth I learned from Jim Rohn when he said, "Be so busy giving others recognition that you don't need it yourself." So try this for yourself. It's ironic that it works. By being busy dispensing praise and recognition to others, I've satisfied my own hunger for it. Here's what I mean . . .

When a teammate achieves something big or small, let's recognize him or her for it. The best way is to recognize that person in front of peers. For example, if you're on a conference call with multiple teammates, you might say, "Guys, I want to recognize Jane. For those who don't know,

Jane had four appointments yesterday! Jane, stellar job! Guys, make sure you congratulate Jane the next time you see her."

Also, recognition can be useful in promoting the exact actions that we want out of our teammates. When we recognize a certain action, we are in essence teaching everyone to repeat that action. If we consistently praise people for setting appointments, we're encouraging a culture of people's setting appointments. So let's be purposeful and selective in what we give recognition to.

Handwritten notes are also effective. My friend Jay Veal, in his book *The Little Book of Network Marketing: A Pocket Guide*, reminded me of the power of handwritten notes. Wow! To say that a hand-written note is powerful is an understatement. Guys, it's huge. A handwritten note is one of the best ways to recognize actions and achievements of your teammates. Making this a part of our culture can be tough. I can't make my teammates write handwritten notes. But I can write them. And my hope is that, over time, I'll create a culture of handwritten notes by my example. It's worth it.

Last, let me say that recognition is separate from promotion. Recognition is its own thing. In your team, create a culture of recognition. Look for individuals who have promoted, sponsored a teammate, or gotten a new customer. Take a minute to recognize them. Your teammates crave recognition and praise. Eagerly look for ways to give it to them. They deserve it.

Personally Sponsoring and Producing

My team has a monthly newsletter, and the only way your name goes in the newsletter is if you personally sponsored (AKA "produced") over the previous thirty days. I designed it this way to motivate my team and to motivate myself. I wanted to use recognition to create a culture of producing. This newsletter is a good way of doing that.

So many of us, myself included, fall into management mode. Ugh. It's so comfortable for us just to teach. It's safe to sit back, help our teammates, and be a supporter. We've got to create a culture of producing. And in our business, we produce by personally sponsoring new teammates and getting new customers.

When I started out, I remember certain calls from my upline, Mike Reid. The calls would go something like this . . .

"Mike, thanks for calling! How are you?"

"Great, David. I'm busy, but I just wanted to tell you that I just sponsored two more people this week!"

"Okay, Mike. Thanks for the call."

"Why is Mike telling me this?" I would wonder. He's my upline. Is he trying to brag? At the time, I was confused.

Now, looking back, I realized exactly what he was doing. He was motivating me. He knew that the best way to teach me what to do was to show me by his own actions. He knew that what he told me meant little, but what he did meant a lot. What a good lesson. I've since realized that people don't watch what we say. They watch what we do.

If we want a culture of production, the only way we'll achieve this is by example. We've got to get out there and produce ourselves. I encourage you to embrace a culture of producing and personally sponsoring; after all, of all the attitudes and characteristics one might embrace, this one pays the best!

6. Promoting

I love this story that Ryan Morris shared with me. Ryan's a friend and phenomenal mentor. Here's what Ryan told me:

"David, before I made it to the level of senior director, my upline leader would call me weekly, and all I would hear was 'senior director, senior director, senior director!' Then he would hang up."

Ryan's leader was effectively instilling a culture of promotion. He was pushing Ryan to make it to the next level.

As human beings, we like playing it safe. We like what's familiar. It takes extra effort for us to stretch outside what's comfortable. For that reason, reaching the next rank can be challenging. It's not natural for us. I think it's important that we, as leaders, decide that the status quo is not okay. "On our team, you promote to the next level! That's what we do!" You would be wise to adapt this phrase as part of your team's culture.

I've heard it said, "If you are not growing, you're dying." I think deep down we all know that's true. If we're not expanding to the next level or rank in our business, then it's likely we're going backward. It seems there is no staying the same. Either we're moving forward or we're moving backward. If that's the case, we might as well move forward. Embrace a culture of promotion on your team. Get that next rank advancement! Celebrate teammates who are promoted. In fact, over-celebrate it! Make it the biggest deal possible. I would dare say that there's no such thing as over-celebrating a promotion.

7. Going to Events

Ask any top leader in your company, and he or she will tell you, "We build this business event to event." To understand why going to events is so vital to success, let's look at what happens at the events.

Events are when someone's hope turns into belief. Typically, it's at an event when a teammate will commit to his or her own success. He makes the decision to go from poser to apprentice. She decides she wants to be a professional. At the events, someone who once was wishy-washy becomes rock solid. Teammates collect stories of others like themselves, and those stories give them hope they didn't have before. Events are masterminds—when teammates share ideas and collaborate with one another. Events are when a teammate's buy-in jumps to a new level.

Again, don't just take my word on this. Go to the top leaders in your company. Ask them, "How important is it to attend big events?" They might even tell you it's the most important thing. I don't disagree. A good team leader builds event to event. A strong team values the events and shows up in big numbers. If attending events becomes a part of your team culture, I can promise you that your results are going to soar!

Here are a few things we can do to help develop events as part of our culture:

- First, get good at communication. Connect early, weeks and months in advance, to find out when and where events will be held, and then communicate this information to your team. Let them know that your team is going. It seems that most conflicts in scheduling can be overcome with good communication about when and where events will be held.

- Second, tell stories of real people who went to a certain event and saw great results afterward. A good example is this: "Hey, guys, Lisa went to last year's Dallas event. She drove ten hours each way! But one year later, Lisa's team of forty is now 400! So let's get our team to Dallas!" Usually a story such as this is much more powerful than any logical reasoning we can offer.

- Third, go yourself. This is obvious, but we still need to mention it. How can you expect your team to go if you don't go? You can't.

- Fourth, establish a more efficient or cost-effective way for your team to attend. For example, if your team is in Atlanta and the event is in Dallas, then organize a bus to lower the travel expenses for your teammates. This is extra work on your part, but sometimes it's necessary to encourage that culture of attending events.

8. Being Involved

Back in college at Auburn University, I would host massive parties. Ask anyone who attended. My parties in college were a blast, even though no alcohol was served. Everyone had a good time. I mean everyone. And the reason was that everyone was involved. Each attendee felt he or she had a purpose. Once, when we did a pumpkin-carving party, hundreds showed up. We made it mandatory that each person had to carve a pumpkin. Everyone was involved, which meant everyone had a blast. I realized back then that simply inviting people to a party was not enough. I had to give them more. I had to get them involved.

The same is true for my church. The church I attended in Auburn, Alabama, had several thousand attendees. When I first went there, I felt like a stranger walking a crowded street. It wasn't until I got involved that I felt as though it was my church.

When people join a networking company, they're likely to leave unless we get them involved. In other words, we want them to be participating somehow as soon as possible. If they don't . . . they won't have fun, they won't be connected, and they're likely to walk out the back door as quickly as they came in the front door.

Here's where your creativity as a leader comes into play. How can you involve your teammates more? How can you get them to participate? Not only how, but also how often? Brainstorm your own ideas about how you can accomplish this within your team. Here are some suggestions to consider.

Team conference calls are great. If at all possible, get your teammates to share ideas and insight on team training calls. I have a nightly volunteer training call that lasts twenty minutes. The first eight minutes, I go over a relevant lesson. The last twelve minutes I open it to teammates sharing their ideas. If you can get your teammates to share ideas in front of others . . . I'd call that involvement.

Team parties are also wonderful. At these parties, set up games and activities that encourages teammates to get involved and to participate. Recently we had a team party called Actors & Appetizers. We asked everyone to bring an appetizer. Then we had an appetizer contest. By everyone bringing an appetizer for the contest, we effectively involved each teammate. There are many other ways to achieve participation when you have team parties.

Starting a book club can effectively achieve involvement. Have teammates summarize different chapters of a particular book. By doing so, you're effectively getting them involved . . . and you'll be surprised by the value they bring to the chapters! I've learned so much from teammates once I got them involved.

Another good way to get others involved is to ask them to share their stories in a group setting. People love to share their stories and they also love hearing other people's stories. Ask teammates to share stories with each other. People feel connected and involved with one another when they know each other better.

CONCLUSION

In conclusion, your team already has a culture. You already have a set of attitudes and behaviors you've adopted either on purpose or by default.

It takes a leader to step up to the plate and create a new team culture. You're that leader. It's up to you. It's not up to your sponsor. It's not up to your company. It's up to you. Take the lead. Be the leader. Be the one who decides what attitudes and behaviors you're going to accept on your team.

To start, write down what your current culture is like. Is it one of apathy like mine was? Write down where you are. Then spend the next hour describing the perfect team culture. Design your team's future. What does it look like? If you can design it, you can achieve it. But it starts with the design. It starts with knowing exactly what core attitudes and behaviors you want to plant in your garden. Plant those attitudes. Plant those behaviors. Weed out the rest.

Eric Worre, author of the *GoPro* series, says, "It takes one year to really establish any aspect of your team's culture." I agree. Your team's culture isn't built overnight. It takes a leader—that's you—knowing what you want and then working hard for a year to instill what you want into your team's culture. It's worth it and you are worth it! I wish the very best for you.

—David Adams

It goes without saying that David Adams has a handle on culture! And believe me, he has the team and the team culture to prove it. Here are a few more thoughts on team building, along with a couple of essential highlights.

USE THE SYSTEM

Team building will require you to expand your focus beyond yourself. Team building is about your helping new associates get their businesses off to a fast start. As you shift your focus to more team building, your skills as a leader will come into play. As your team starts to grow, it is more important than ever to follow your company's system. Make sure everything you do can be duplicated by everyone on your team. Consistent duplication of the system is essential for explosive growth and massive success.

This is the cycle of duplication that you want your team to use:

- Sponsor new associates.
- Teach them your system.
- Help them get started.
- Repeat over and over.

In a perfect world, team building would involve building our front lines and teaching them to build their front lines, and on and on. We recruit joiners to find leaders. We look for leaders who will find other leaders who will find other leaders. It's not so much about how many associates you have on your team, but how many leaders you have on your team. The more people who we sponsor and teach, the more leaders we will find, the bigger our team will grow, and the larger our income will be. The bottom line is that we will sort through lots of duds to find a few studs.

> *"A great manager has a knack for making ballplayers think they are better than they are."*
>
> **—REGGIE JACKSON**

MEETING AFTER THE MEETING

The meetings after the meetings are critical. When the formal business presentation is over, circle your team up in a corner, and spend time with them. Another way to create team chemistry is to go out to eat with your team, or go to a coffee shop after the meeting. Spending time with your team and creating team culture is very important. It creates synergy, which helps create momentum on your team.

BELIEVE IN YOUR TEAM

Always be positive when talking to your downline. Negativity is a cancer. A few positive words can do amazing things. There are many people in network marketing who are successful for one main reason: someone believed in them more than they believed in themselves. Someone gave them positive strokes. The power of someone's believing in them gave them enough push to find success. In networking, one of the most important leadership attributes is to believe in your team even more than they believe in themselves.

RECOGNITION

Everyone has a natural desire to feel that he or she is *somebody*. This desire to be important is our most compelling non-biological hunger, and recognition is our most sought-after reward. As I have heard Randy Hedge say many times, "Babies cry for it and grown men die for it." No other business provides the recognition we receive in networking. Nothing in the networking business is more fulfilling than when new networkers thank us for giving them the opportunities that changed their lives.

Everyone has a need for approval. Everyone wants to be recognized. Your team will soon realize that they are going to work harder than they ever imagined. But there is a window there, and the harder they work, the wider the window of opportunity opens. In turn, they will make more money, and they will receive more recognition. As leaders, we must reinforce good performance by praising deserving associates in front of their peers. Make sure to reinforce large and small accomplishments. If the associate gets one new customer, make a big deal out of it. Not only do associates want to feel that what they are doing is important, they want to know their efforts are appreciated.

CONFERENCE CALLS

Conference calls are a great way to inspire the team and share information about upcoming events and promotions. They are also a fantastic tool for offering tips and basic training. Conference calls can create urgency among associates, new and old alike. They are a great way to stimulate activity.

Doing special conference calls with your leaders is important. It makes them feel special. Make participation in the leadership conference calls contingent on reaching certain leadership levels. People don't want to feel left out and will climb big walls to be on leadership calls.

ATTEND ALL BIG EVENTS

I believe that every great leader in network marketing had his or her fire fully lit at a big event. Just as I shared earlier in the book, my turning point came at a national event. Many others have had similar experiences. It's easy to understand once you have experienced big events and the culture that they create.

Big events raise the belief level of those who attend. A person's willingness to commit to building his or her business is always determined by individual level. If you were to interview the top network marketers from around the world, you would be amazed to learn how many leaders saw the light at a big event.

We build our teams from big event to big event. This has come to be called "event culture" by some. It raises people's awareness that what they have become a part of is bigger than they are. They look on stage and see people who look like they do, and they start realizing that success is within reach!

You can't expect your team to attend and promote big events if you don't attend and promote them. So, create event culture within your group. Make a commitment to your company's big events, and it will pay huge dividends.

COACH'S FOUR RULES FOR BIG EVENTS

I just mentioned that we build event to event. All great leaders in networking are promoters. They're always promoting the next big event as the biggest event in company history—because it is! But as soon as that event is over, these experienced leaders begin hyping the next big event as the biggest ever in company history—because it is! And this process never ends. You see, strong leaders understand that belief, inspiration, duplication, and commitment are the results of attending big events.

So it's worth repeating: network marketing is built event to event! To help you do this, here are four simple rules you can follow.

RULE #1 – YOU GO.

Even when no one else is going, you must go. You now know the value of big events. You recognize that, even if you're attending alone, the big event is where the magic happens. It's where your belief rises. It's where you commit. Sure, you might feel like an ugly duckling as you sit in the shadows while the swans walk the stage. But it's in those lonely emotional moments when you make a promise to yourself, "Never again! Soon these people will know my name! Soon my family will be proud of me! Next time, it's me who walks the stage!"

RULE #2 – DON'T GO ALONE.

Now that you've decided to attend, next you need to decide that you won't go alone. This is easier to do once you've followed Rule #1. The word "let's" is the word you can now employ. "Sue, let's go together!" Or, "John, let's go to Dallas!" Or, "Joe, let's go together to Orlando!" The word let's is powerful. Remember, you're going! You must have this mindset: "I'm going whether you go or not." This leadership mindset shows your commitment and attracts others. Therefore, you must follow Rule #1 before you can expect to have success with Rule #2. And make it fun! Big events are a blast! As you compel your teammates to attend, remind them of the fun you're going to have together! For me, big events rank right up there with Christmas! It's a blast to be around like-minded people, everyone going in the same direction.

RULE #3 – WALK THE STAGE.

There's no feeling like walking the stage in front of thousands of people. Sure, the money in networking is great, but those moments of recognition seem almost priceless. No other profession is better at recognition than the profession of network marketing. Big events are a time for recognition. It's likely that your next big event is a month or two away. So find out what you need to do to walk the stage at your next big event. What rank must you promote to? How many customers are required? How many associates must you sponsor? Find out what it takes. Use the event date as your deadline. Let it force you to do what it takes. Accept no excuse. Refuse anything less. Every day, between now and your next big event, visualize yourself walking that stage. See yourself in the spotlight with all eyes on you! Envision it clearly. Feel the feeling, as if you're walking the stage now. This vision will drive your efforts. "I can. I will. I must!" That is now your mindset.

RULE #4 – HELP OTHERS WALK THE STAGE.

The only feeling better than your walking the stage is helping others walk the stage. It feels wonderful to know that you had a hand in their success. You feel proud. You see the joy in their eyes. You see their confidence and belief in their own abilities rise. You're watching their lives begin to change. And you had something to do with it. Decide today that you will help at least one other teammate walk the stage at your next big event. Paint this vision for him. Help her see it clearly in advance. Write out a road map of what it will take to reach the next rank advancement. Then come up with a plan. I can tell you that all my success has come from helping others advance in rank, helping others to walk the stage, and helping others to grab the spotlight. Jim Rohn says it best: "Be so busy giving other people recognition that you really don't need it for yourself." The secret to network marketing might be found in those few words!

 Edify your top associates and encourage team newcomers with a callout on your own social media. Use #CoachPresley on your Facebook and Twitter.

HOMEWORK

For anything to happen, you must do it twice: once in your mind and once in reality. The purpose of this exercise is to help you create a vision for your team (doing it in your mind) so that you can move forward to make it a reality.

1. Take some time to think about every aspect of the team—the organization you're starting to create. Create the ideal team in your imagination.

2. Write down a description of your ideal team using a pen and paper. This is important! Not only are you imagining your team here, you are actually designing your future! So don't cheat your future by shortcutting this exercise. Here are some questions to help you think and create a clear vision for your team:

   - Do I have a team name?
   - How big is my team at this time next year? In five years?
   - How many of my teammates will attend the next big event with me?

- How does my team interact with one another?
- How do I communicate with the group?
- What can we do to get the new person paid quickly?
- What standards will I set as the leader?
- What activities do we prohibit on our team?
- In what ways do we keep it all simple?
- In what ways do we encourage personal development?
- What can make us unique as a group?
- What activities should we celebrate? And how?
- How do we make this business the most fun?
- What is a compelling mission that our team can rally behind?

3. These are questions to get your mind flowing and your pen moving. Just imagine your team in the future. Design it on paper. Write it out. Envision your group. See yourself at the next big event. Give your vision color. Then add your emotions to the scene, the feelings you will feel when your team is all around you. You'll find that doing this will help you create more clarity and a more compelling vision for your future team.

4. Describe your vision in a Tweet and on your Facebook wall. Make sure your team sees it! And include #CoachPresley and post them to my Facebook wall www.facebook.com/presleyswagerty for me and others to see and support you as well.

So in closing, remember this order: Vision → Effort → Results. The vision you have for your future compels your highest effort, and that effort leads to your results. But it starts with your vision.

CHAPTER 19 – Every Team Needs a Captain

"Leadership is not about titles, positions, or flowcharts. It is about one life influencing another."

—John C. Maxwell

In this chapter, you will find out that anyone can be a leader because all leadership means is that you can influence others. A leader helps people change their mindsets and actions for the better. Show me any organization that is exploding, and I will show you a leader at the top of that organization.

In networking, we lead a volunteer army, and it requires a higher level of leadership than traditional businesses, because there are no formal lines of authority. We are not our team's boss. We cannot fire them. In short, we can't make them do anything. A leader in networking is more like a team captain or a player–coach who leads by example.

THE ULTIMATE PLAYER–COACH

No one led by example better than Hall of Fame NBA player Bill Russell did. He was the cornerstone of the Boston Celtics' dynasty of the 1960s. His many individual accolades were well deserved, but they were only products of Russell's commitment to team play. His greatest accomplishment was bringing the storied Celtics eleven championships in his thirteen seasons.

As Celtics player Don Nelson told the *Boston Herald*,

> *"There are two types of superstars. One makes himself look good at the expense of the other guys on the floor. But there's another type who makes the players around him look better than they are, and that's the type Russell was."*

— **DON NELSON**

During the Russell era, it became clear that basketball was a team game. As Russell later wrote:

> *"To me, one of the most beautiful things to see is a group of men coordinating their efforts toward a common goal, alternately subordinating and asserting themselves to achieve real teamwork in action. I tried to do that, we all tried to do that, on the Celtics. I think we succeeded."*

— **BILL RUSSELL**

A dynasty was established under Red Auerbach, and "Boston Celtics" and "NBA champions" became practically synonymous. The team was multitalented, with many great players, but Russell was the cornerstone. With individual greatness, awesome stats, and a Hall of Fame career, I think the role Russell played as a leader during his player–coach days speaks volumes.

Following another NBA championship in 1965–66, Red Auerbach retired, and Russell took over as player–coach the following season. He led Boston to a 60–21 regular-season record his first year as the coach. His second year coaching, Boston returned to form, recapturing the championship. In the Eastern Division Final, the club came back from trailing by two games to force a seventh game with the 76ers. The Celtics were leading 97–95 with thirty-four seconds left in the game, when Russell took over. He nailed a foul shot, blocked a shot, grabbed a rebound, and—ever the team player—fed the game-winning assist to teammate Sam Jones, who made the final basket in a 100–96 triumph. Boston beat Los Angeles in six games to be champions again.

The 1968–69 season was even more electrifying. The Celtics, showing their age, barely made it into the playoffs. But they caught fire in the postseason. In Russell's third year as player–coach, Boston repeated their role as NBA champions by defeating the Lakers in a seven-game battle. The great Celtics leader promptly retired, having guided the team to eleven championships in thirteen years. Russell had amassed 21,620 career rebounds, second in NBA history.

One of the game's greatest players, Bill Russell personified servant leadership: leading by example, with the will to win.

COACH'S SUCCESS TIP:

LEAD BY EXAMPLE. DO WHAT YOU WANT YOUR TEAM TO DO.

A team captain is a leader whose inclination is first to serve, not to lead. It is the desire to serve that creates the leader. Leaders have a caring persona. They care about all members of the organization and their successes. They genuinely want personal and professional growth, not just for themselves, but also for their teams.

The process of putting others first is realizing that not everything is about you. In The Power of Ethical Management, Ken Blanchard and Norman Vincent Peale wrote, "People with humility don't think less of themselves, they just think of themselves less."

Leaders should be characterized by humility and a desire to share the spotlight. Leaders should give credit to others when possible. Leaders understand that associates work harder and with more focus when they are recognized for their contributions to the team.

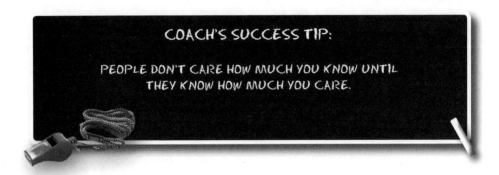

COACH'S SUCCESS TIP:

PEOPLE DON'T CARE HOW MUCH YOU KNOW UNTIL
THEY KNOW HOW MUCH YOU CARE.

10 STEPS TO LEADERSHIP

1. **You must make no small plans.** As leaders, we are in the dream business. We must see things differently. We must see things as they can be and not as they are. Leaders show that dreams can become a reality with hard work, while so many others work hard to block out the reality that they really have no dreams. We must get our team in the dream business again. Dreams enrich your life by giving it hope and direction. One of the greatest benefits of networking is getting to associate with people who have dreams.

2. **You must care about your team.** Leaders must want to make a difference in the lives of others. As a leader, you must get to know the people on your team. To lead people and to motivate people they must first know that you care. As the old saying goes, "People don't care how much you know until they know how much you care." Get lost in the success of your team. Zig Ziglar tells us, "You can have everything in life you want, if you will just help enough other people get what they want."

3. **You must lead by example.** This is a monkey see, monkey do business. You do what you want your team to do. Leaders must get in the trenches, and their teams will follow. If you want prospects and new associates to be excited about your business, then you need to be excited about your business. If you are at a 2-on-1, sit on the edge of your seat and be engaged. If you are at a home meeting watching a DVD presentation, act as if it is the best movie you have ever seen. If you are at a big meeting, sit toward the front of the room, stay focused, and act as though it's the first time you have seen the presentation. Too many times, I see leaders who stand outside or sit in the back of the room looking bored. This sets the wrong example. It makes it look like the leader is no longer

fired up and excited about the business. Always remember that there is a direct correlation between what leaders do and what their teams do. I remember a few years ago when I started showing the plan using a black, three-ringed binder. About a month after I started showing it that way, I was at a hotel meeting, and I looked around the room. Much to my surprise, many in the room were holding a black, three-ringed binder. Modeling is powerful. Model what you want your team to do. If you want your team to be excited . . . you be excited. If you want your team to attend meetings . . . you attend meetings. If you want your team to show the plan . . . you show the plan. If you want your team to make money . . . you make money. Don't wait for a leader . . . you be the leader.

4. **You must have commitment.** What is commitment? It is an unwavering belief. It is a state of mind. It is an attitude that failure is not an option. You need that inner "want to" that keeps you up at night. I've found that people want to stick their toe in the water and say that when they start making big money, they will jump in . . . WRONG! If you don't jump in, you will never make big money. One of the key steps to being a great leader is total commitment. You must make the decision that you want to change your life. Then, you must reinforce that decision by plugging into meetings, reading good books, listening to good CDs, and hanging with committed people until your decision becomes a commitment. With a true commitment, you can change the world . . . you can certainly change your financial picture.

5. **You must set goals.** There is power in writing your goals down with a date. Your mind is then aware of them and gets to work achieving your goals.

6. **You must be success motivated.** Generating resources leads to bigger possibilities in your life. Money gives you options that broke people will never have.

7. **You must be coachable.** Don't try to reinvent the wheel. Follow the proven plan. Ask yourself, "Who has done what I want to do?" It is important to hang out with people who have what you want; they have the map.

8. **You must be a team player.**
   T – Together
   E – Everyone
   A – Achieves
   M – More

9. **You must have a "now" mentality.** How many people do you know who say, "Someday, when my ship comes in . . . Someday, when I have the time . . . Someday, when I have the money . . . Someday, when I learn the skills . . ." Have I got some shocking news for you! Someday doesn't exist, never has, and never will. There is only today. Yesterday is history. Tomorrow is a mystery. Today is all we have. As a leader, you must have a willingness to act. Recognizing opportunity and acting on it is a key trait of a true leader. How many of us have been at the right place at the right time, but it took hindsight for us to realize it? There is no time like the present to get the job done. Do it now!

10. **You must never quit.** Perseverance is the key. When the going gets tough, the tough get going. They don't quit. Leaders dream big, work hard, and see the job through.

COACH'S SUCCESS TIP:

LEADERS DREAM BIG, WORK HARD, AND SEE THE JOB THROUGH.

In networking, I believe we are leading a crusade against debt and financial worries. Our motivation in networking goes beyond money. It's about growing as a person, making friends, and helping people. Unfortunately, far too many people work only for money and don't have their heart in their work. The need to earn a living often overshadows the calling we have, so much so that people will work at jobs they hate. Leaders in networking push themselves to achieve beyond their own or anyone else's expectations.

Leadership also involves your ability to pass your passion and enthusiasm to others. Approaching your networking business with dedication is not enough. You must inspire others. You have to radiate your commitment to your business so that your enthusiasm is contagious to your team.

You have to let your team know where you stand, what the dream means to you, and what you are willing to do to make it come true. The leader must be committed to the success of everyone on the team. The leader helps the team grow and coaches them on how to improve their skills to achieve their dreams.

As the team captain, selling the future—the potential success of the team and each associate is also your job.

I have covered the how-tos in this book, but they mean nothing without a huge "want to!" If you want to badly enough, you will figure out how. That has been proven time and again by so many top earners.

The only qualification I have to be a multimillionaire is how badly I wanted to succeed, and it all happened in spite of the odds. I grew up poor and coached basketball for sixteen years, and I wouldn't change a thing because all of those experiences are what have allowed me to be where I am today.

Because of networking, we have a chance to make a difference in our world. It happens one person at a time, as we touch the lives of other people. Because of the exponential growth that is possible in networking, before we realize it, we may have touched the lives of thousands, and our dreams can become our reality.

I'm convinced with all my heart that there will be two kinds of people when it comes to networking as a vehicle for financial freedom: 1) those who wish they had and 2) those who are glad they did. I hope that you will be in the "glad they did" category!

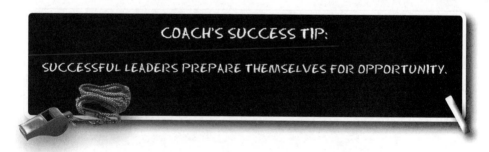

COACH'S SUCCESS TIP:

SUCCESSFUL LEADERS PREPARE THEMSELVES FOR OPPORTUNITY.

HOMEWORK

The fact that you've made it to the end of this book tells me that you're special. You're unique. Many buy the book, but only a special few ever finish it. Celebrate yourself and the fact that you're one of the few who finish!

But your journey as a leader in networking is just beginning. Your team needs you to step up as the captain. And to be a captain, you must be a strong leader. So let's take a moment to do personal inventory on your leadership ability. The 10 Steps to Leadership were detailed earlier in this chapter. Here they are again:

10 Steps to Leadership

1) You must make no small plans.

2) You must care about your team.

3) You must lead by example.

4) You must be committed.

5) You must set goals.

6) You must be success motivated.

7) You must be coachable.

8) You must be a team player.

9) You must have a "now" mentality.

10) You must never quit.

1. Review each step. Write them down on a sheet of paper.

2. Next to each step, write out how you can improve in that specific area. In which of the ten are you doing well? Applaud yourself in these areas.

3. Keep this list with you. Review these 10 Steps and revisit how you're doing in each.

4. Post these steps to Twitter or Facebook, one a day, with a brief statement of how you plan to implement it. Include #CoachPresley.

Next, find two or three people on your team, and share this list with them. If you're just beginning, share this list with two to three people you love and respect. Compliment them on the steps where you believe they excel. Suggest to them that they do a self-inventory, as you have done. Finally, ask these individuals to lend you their critical feedback, in reference to the 10 Steps. Where do they think you need the most improvement? Which steps do they see as your areas of strength? Feedback is the breakfast of champions. You're looking for as much feedback as possible to be the champion leader you know you can be!

While every step is important, I believe that steps 1 and 4 could be the most important. You must be committed. And you must dream big! If you're truly committed, and you have a strong compelling dream, you'll soon find the other steps will align beautifully for you.

Dream big. Commit. And I can't wait to hear your story of success!

Visit www.PresleySwagerty.com for daily coaching tips. I'm here with you to help you achieve your dreams!

All the best,

Presley

Epilogue

Although today I live just a few miles from 8724 Dunlap Drive, my lifestyle seems light years away from the two-bedroom home in which my mom raised me. My only regret about the amazing life I have been blessed with is that it did not happen just a few years earlier. You see, I can still remember my mom sitting on the couch, counting out change from the bottom of her purse to see whether she had enough money to go eat a hamburger with a friend. When I was coaching, I helped her out when I could, but my life was a struggle as well. If success had come along a little sooner, my mom would have been shopping 'til she dropped, driving a Mercedes, and eating at the finest restaurants.

The sad irony for me is that right around the time Jeanie and I started making serious money, my little mama's mind started slipping. However, because I was willing to be different and make a change, I didn't have to put my mom into a nursing home because that is what the government would pay for. I was able to care for her in an assisted living facility, where she could live with some dignity. My mom died February 6, 2008, and it was the saddest day of my life. I still miss her, but I focus on my family and our business and everything is okay. Mom would be proud of our accomplishments.

Today, we have options. When Jordan decided to play baseball at Arizona State, Jeanie and I bought a home there. It is a 7,000-square-foot home that sits on the South Mountain range. When Jordan was asked to play ball in the Cape Cod League over the summer, we rented a house in New England and watched every game. Recently, when a great deal came along on a 13,000-square-foot estate on forty acres overlooking Lake Grapevine, we were able to buy what, just a few years ago, I would have seen as a mansion of epic proportions, well out of reach for a poor boy from Pleasant Grove.

It's funny how life can seem like it's in slow motion. I remember it like it was yesterday: my cousin Rhonda and I cruising Buckner Boulevard in Aunt Ruby's '63 Buick LeSabre, thinking life couldn't get any better. Today, we own a luxury car collection ranging from Mercedes-Benzes and BMWs to Dodge Vipers and Hummers. They are a far cry from that '63 Buick we could only park in certain parking spaces because, in disrepair, it wouldn't go in reverse.

Today, something I am proud of is that our success has affected others. My cousin Manny Carter was the one who taught me the importance of taking a stance so others see they can. Obviously, I am proud that my actions have had an impact on thousands of people financially through our company.

I am most proud, however, of our two children. Our daughter SaraBeth was an all-state singer, and I rarely missed a show. Her lifelong dream was to attend Baylor University, and there was no way that I could have afforded that on a coach's salary. However, because of our networking business, SaraBeth was able to attend Baylor. The rest of the story is that she, by building her own networking business, was able to pay her own way the last three years. She graduated with a 3.9 GPA from the Baylor business school. She has a residual income through her networking business that most adults would dream of for a salary and, more importantly, she has options. At 23, she bought her first house, a beautiful 3,500-square-foot home in an upscale neighborhood, which is far from a starter home. She also drives a new Mercedes. Because she has a residual income, SaraBeth is able to pursue her recording career. She is working on her first country music album with her producer, Dean Sams of the iconic group *Lone Star*. You can hear her music at www.SaraBethMusic.com. I could not be more proud of everything she has accomplished. I am more excited about what lies ahead for her. SaraBeth thinks differently from most twenty-four-year-olds: she is looking at business deals and figuring out different ways to expand her possibilities. She's able to dream big and reach for the stars.

When he was growing up, our son was just like me. His passion for athletics was evident at a very early age. At three years old, Jordan was playing T-ball with four- and five-year-olds. He excelled at every sport that he played. But, as he entered high school, it became apparent that baseball was where his best prospects were. As a freshman, Jordan attended Garland High School, where baseball was an afterthought. The field looked like an old cow pasture with a couple of bases and a backstop. It killed me that I couldn't send him to a private school where he could flourish in both academics and athletics. By his sophomore year, our financial picture had begun to change, and we were able to enroll him at Prestonwood Christian Academy. Prestonwood is a great academic school and has one of the top baseball programs in Texas. I don't know what his future would have held if that hadn't happened. However, it didn't hurt being at a school with first-class facilities and a talented coach, Mike Maack. At Prestonwood, the college coaches and professional scouts visited regularly.

As Jordan progressed, he was offered scholarships all over the country, and he decided to attend Arizona State University, one of the nation's top college baseball programs. ASU went to the College World Series both years Jordan played there. By his sophomore year, he was an All-American, and the pro scouts were calling. Jordan was drafted in the second round of the MLB draft by the St. Louis Cardinals and is living out the dream of every boy who has ever strapped on a pair of cleats.

The thing that I am probably most grateful for is the time freedom. Randy Hedge is famous for saying, "There is a difference between making a living and making a life." I have a life, and I love it. I can count on one hand the times that I have missed one of Jordan's baseball games or SaraBeth's performances.

For the past seven years, I have owned my own time. I have had no boss to tell me what to do, no supervisor to check in with, and no overhead to keep me up at night. As I enter the halftime of life, my life is nothing short of a dream. In fact, my reality now is better than my dreams used to be. Never could I have imagined—as I was growing up on Dunlap—all that life has to offer. I urge you not to settle. No matter what's in your past, you can start now changing your future. None of us can go back and make a new beginning, but we can all start now and make a new ending. I urge you to keep dreaming and, most important, keep working and aspiring to be, do, and have more.

Coach's Q & A

What if my spouse isn't interested?

Don't let that stop you. A lot of the time only one spouse initially gets the business started. Once the business starts having success, the other spouse will usually get involved.

Should I work with associates below my first level?

Yes. We obviously focus on our personal recruits and the associates closest to us, but we should help everyone in our organization. When you work down in your group, you are building a foundation and putting heat under associates who are in higher levels.

Is it a pyramid?

No. The biggest difference between network marketing and pyramids is that pyramids are illegal. I believe that when someone asks if it is a pyramid, they are really asking if your business is legal and the answer is "yes." Networking has been around for decades and if it were illegal, it would have been shut down years ago.

My sponsor doesn't help me. What should I do?

Go upline until you find someone who will help you. Also, stay plugged in to local meetings and trainings. Many times you can find associates willing to help who aren't in your upline. This is a helping business.

How important are the meetings after the meetings?

I think connecting with your team is very important and going out for coffee or a meal after the meeting is a great way to accomplish that. People like to know that they are part of something bigger than themselves. Also, anytime you do something to bring your team together, you are creating energy.

What if I just don't have the time?

First and foremost, we make time for what we think is important in our lives. Also, I usually ask the prospects what they are doing to get their time back. If I'm dealing with someone who is very busy, I simply say this: "I'm not asking for your time, only your contacts. You make a call of introduction and I will show the plan. In other words, we will use your contacts and my time. Put me to work for you."

Can I work more than one network marketing program at the same time?

No. I don't believe you can chase more than one rabbit at a time. I think we can look like "snake oil salesmen" if we offer multiple opportunities at the same time. If you are focused on making life-changing income with your new business, it will take up all of your available time.

What if my prospect says, "I can't afford to get into your business"?

A person can get started in most network marketing companies for under $400. If your prospect can't scratch up a little money to join your team, they really need your business . . . unless they want to spend the rest of their life working for someone else.

What if the prospect says, "I had a bad experience in networking. The company I was with went bankrupt"?

This would be like buying a car that was a lemon and deciding you were never going to drive again. Another example would be getting a bad meal at a restaurant and deciding that all restaurants must be bad. If your company fails, find another one. Never quit!

Coach, I really want to do this, but I just can't seem to get it going. What should I do?

Anything significant that we do in life, we must do twice, once in our mind and once for real. We have to make a decision that we are going to change our lives with networking, no matter what.

Then we must take action. Get out of your comfort zone and talk to people. It's that simple. Follow your company's system and stay consistent and persistent. The skills you need to be a success come from practice. Practice comes from overcoming your fear and nothing is better for overcoming fear than taking action. Action will take you out of doubt, but doubt will take you out of action. Stay in the game!

What's the single most important thing I can do to ensure my success?

Successful networkers know that their success is a direct result of helping others be successful. They get great pleasure and satisfaction from watching others change their lives. Pour yourself into the success of others, your team, and your success will be a given.

How can I make my meetings stand apart?

Network marketing companies and the field should always keep meetings consistent. Any prospect should be able to attend any meeting in any city and get the same information.

I find it awkward to ask someone to join at the end of my presentations. What do I do?

I like the following acronym: ABC-Always Be Closing.

After your prospect sees a business presentation, ask the prospect to join your team. There are really only three answers that you will hear: yes, no, and maybe. Yes is great. When they say yes, get to a computer and get them signed up in the business. We love it when the prospect says yes.

No is okay, too. When the prospect says no, try to get them to be your customer and ask if you can contact them in six months and tell them how your business is going.

The maybes are the ones that will drive you crazy. Maybe usually comes out as "I need to think about it," "I need to pray about it," "I need to talk to my spouse," etc. When they give me a maybe, I always say the same thing, "Great! You think about it, and I will call you tomorrow, and you let me know what you have decided." "Great! You pray about it, and I will call you tomorrow, and you let me know what you have decided." "Great! You talk to your spouse, and I will call you tomorrow, and you let me know what you have decided." Just fill in the blank, and let them know you will be calling tomorrow.

If they are still undecided when I call the next day, I simply ask them to be my customer and move them to my follow-up list. I don't waste time on indecisive people. Your success depends on moving forward and simply showing the plan to someone else as quickly as you can.

Who should I look to for help and advice?

Get a mentor. Follow a proven leader.

New associates need to use their upline, when possible, but you can be successful without upline support. It is much more important for you to be supportive.

Say nothing – Do nothing – Be nothing.

Be the leader for your downline that you wish you had. Or if you have a great sponsor, emulate them. Bottom line, be the leader you want your teammates to become.

Coach, what's the best way to handle objections?

Objections more often than not are excuses. One of the biggest excuses people give for not joining our team is . . . "I don't have the time." When I hear this, I tell them, "Busy people make the best associates." Then ask: "What are you doing to get your time back?"

Another excuse is "I don't have the money." When one of my prospects tells me this, I say, "Then you really need this and I can help you. Let me show you, with a little effort, how fast you can have your money back in your pocket." When I think of objections or excuses, the advice of my best friend, Randy Hedge, comes to mind. Randy always says, "If someone says they aren't a salesperson, I say let's go find three salespeople. If they say they don't have credibility, I say find three that do. If they insist they don't have any time, then find three with the time." You get the idea.

Your Game Plan Reading List

Beach Money by Jordan Adler

Business of the 21st Century by Robert Kiyosaki

The Greatest Networker in the World by John Fogg

The Lotus Code by Mark Yarnell and Valerie Bates

Mach II with Your Hair on Fire by Richard Brooke

Making the First Circle Work by Randy Gage

MLM Blueprint by Kody Bateman

Networking Times Magazine

Network Marketing Straight Talk by George Zalucki

Plan C: A Proven Path to Financial Freedom by Glenn Head

Resolved Primer by Orrin Woodward and John David Mann

The Next Millionaires by Paul Zane Pilzer

The Slight Edge by Jeff Olson

Think and Grow Rich by Napoleon Hill

Your Best Year in Network Marketing by Mark Yarnell

Visit my website www.presleyswagerty.com for additional resources to help you build your business.

Acknowledgments

Writing a book may seem to be an individual project, but nothing could be further from the truth. The reality is that if you want it to be read by millions of people, it takes a team. The first and most important team in anyone's life is family.

I'd first like to thank the love of my life, my wife Jeanie. Mere words cannot express my gratitude to her for her love, support, and encouragement during the writing of this book. Without her, I could not have written this book. She is an amazing woman, and I thank the Lord for her every day.

Next, I want to thank my daughter SaraBeth and my son Jordan. I am so excited that they are both pursuing their dreams. They are very talented, and I couldn't ask for two better kids. They are my pride and joy.

I'd also like to thank my in-laws, Bob and Delores Young, for treating me like one of their kids. They are the absolute best.

To my best friend, Randy Hedge—thanks for being in my life.

Thanks to John C. Maxwell for encouraging me to write a book. He got the wheels turning.

Thank you to my friend Jay Veal for his assistance and encouragement.

Another big thank-you goes to Chris LaFaive for his help in so many areas of my life. He is a great friend and a talented individual.

Finally, thanks to the numerous networkers who have touched our lives for the past twenty years. You are destined to change lives and to lead the way for the growing number of people seeking a different lifestyle. We are proud to be involved in this incredible profession with you.

About the Author

As one of the country's leading speakers and authors on attaining financial independence and wealth, Presley Swagerty tells his story, which began with the humblest of roots before transforming into a true American success story.

A self-made multimillionaire, well-respected businessman, success coach, speaker, and author, Presley grew up with his mom in an impoverished area of Dallas and, in his formative years, used basketball as an anchor to keep him on the right track in life. He earned his bachelor's degree in history and math and became a successful high school basketball coach over a sixteen-year career. Along the way, he earned the fitting nickname of "Coach," a title he proudly wears today as he continues mentoring and coaching thousands of people to take the next step toward living their dreams. After coaching, Presley developed into one of the world's leading networkers, building a distributor force of over 250,000 independent associates.

Coach lives out his personal motto of "Be, Do, and Have More," as he motivates and equips people around the world to do the same. The secret to success is not where one is raised, as Coach's story proves; it is the drive and motivation that exists within an individual to get to whatever the next desired level might be. This is a frequently delivered message, complete with instructional how-tos, when Coach speaks as a keynote presenter at workshops and before audiences of thousands at major national conferences.

Coach's straight-from-the-heart, high-energy, passionate message motivates and engages audiences to step into their greatness, providing them with the motivation to take the next steps toward living their dreams. His charisma, warmth, and sense of humor have affected thousands upon thousands of lives.

Among his other endeavors, Presley is a successful businessman with a vast and varied portfolio. He is a major shareholder for Global Innovation, where he serves on the board of directors. He also owns real estate company Swagerty

Investments, record label Circle S Records, and music publishing company Delta Pearl Publishing.

Coach and his wife Jeanie live in Flower Mound, Texas. They have two successful, grown children, SaraBeth and Jordan, who have displayed the same desire to succeed as their dad. SaraBeth is a rapidly rising star in the country music industry and has released her first full-length CD, *Anything is Possible*. Jordan is a talented, professional baseball pitcher for the St. Louis Cardinals organization.

Among his hobbies and personal interests, Coach enjoys spending time with family and friends, watching Jordan play baseball, attending SaraBeth's concerts, traveling, playing golf, and working out.

He has experienced the depths of financial despair and achieved the pinnacle of wealth. His success story comes with a proven blueprint to share with anyone seeking a major change in life. Make this your own personal opportunity to "Be, Do, and Have More."